CW00371374

"You can observe a

—Yogi Berra

"A fool and his money are lucky enough
to get together in the first place."

—Gordon Gekko, *Wall Street*

"If you drink too much from a bottle
marked 'poison,' it is almost certain
to disagree with you, sooner or later."

—*Alice in Wonderland*

"Fool me once, shame on you.
Fool me twice, shame on me.
Fool me three times?
Wait, what were we talking about?"

—Michael Craig

T H E

5 Minute

INVESTOR

When You Don't Want to Spend the Time, But Want the Results

 Michael Craig

CAREER
PRESS

Franklin Lakes, NJ

Copyright © 2002 by Michael Craig

All rights reserved under the Pan-American and International Copyright Conventions. This book may not be reproduced, in whole or in part, in any form or by any means electronic or mechanical, including photocopying, recording, or by any information storage and retrieval system now known or hereafter invented, without written permission from the publisher, The Career Press.

THE 5 MINUTE INVESTOR
Edited by Dianna Walsh
Typeset by Eileen Dow Munson
Cover design by Design Concept
Printed in the U.S.A. by Book-mart Press

To order this title, please call toll-free 1-800-CAREER-1 (NJ and Canada: 201-848-0310) to order using VISA or MasterCard, or for further information on books from Career Press.

The Career Press, Inc., 3 Tice Road, PO Box 687,
Franklin Lakes, NJ 07417
www.careerpress.com

Library of Congress Cataloging-in-Publication Data

Craig, Michael, 1958-
    The 5 minute investor : when you don't want to spend the time, but want the results / by Michael Craig.
        p. cm.
    Includes bibliographical references and index.
    ISBN 1-56414-627-8 (paper)
        1. Corporation reports. 2. Corporation reports—United States. 3. Financial statements.
    4. Financial statements—United States. I. Title: Five minute investor. II. Title.

    HG4028.B2 C73 2002
    332.63'2042—dc21

                                                                            2002073367

Acknowledgments

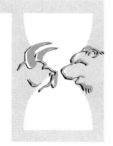

To Jo Anne, an asset of infinite value, still unimpaired after all these years.

To Barry, Ellie, and Valerie.

To Ken Kurson, for his friendship and encouragement, and for improving the proposal for this book.

To the inattentive and irresponsible folks at Enron, Waste Management, Arthur Andersen, Global Crossing, KPMG, Dollar General, Xerox, General Electric, Ernst & Young, Cendant, PriceWaterhouse Coopers, Lucent, IBM, Cisco, MicroStrategy, McKesson HBOC, Deloitte & Touche, and the rest. Thank you for making this book necessary.

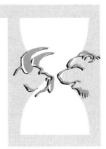

Contents

Part III. The Income Statement
83

Part IV. The Balance Sheet...and Beyond
167

Money, Brains, and Enron

No one should write an investment book these days without addressing Enron. Fortunately, one of the reasons I wrote this book is to teach you how to avoid companies that lie, mislead, or fail to inform investors about their financial condition. As much as I'd like to see Congress and the **Securities and Exchange Commission (SEC)** require better disclosures, and see companies voluntarily disclose more information, I am disappointed that no one has suggested that investors take more responsibility. (A note about definitions: When I use a term for the first time in this book, I will note it in bold print. If it becomes the focus of a later chapter, and I think there is a chance I haven't yet completely explained the term, I will place it in bold print again. All such terms will be defined in the Glossary.) Amid all the finger-pointing and chest-thumping by legislators and commentators, everyone just assumes that investors are powerless to protect themselves from deceitful, dishonest, and even shady companies.

I'm disappointed, but not surprised. I used to represent defrauded investors, and it is important that the laws offer as much investor protection as possible, not just for the investors but also for capital formation. If people think the game is rigged, they are going to flee the stock market. But it is taken as an article of faith that, because Enron fooled regulators, analysts, and the entire community of **institutional investors**, individual investors had no chance to do better.

That's just not so. You can get any public company's **financial statements** for free from numerous sources. The financial statements consist of the **income statement, balance sheet, cash flow statement**, and narrative (**management's discussion and analysis of operations (MD&A)** and **footnotes**). The purpose of this book is to show you how, in as little as five minutes, you can find out information about a company that is more valuable than anything you previously knew.

If I want to cut through the complexity of a company's financial statements, I look first at the cash flow statement for **operating cash flow**. Operating cash flow is the net amount of cash provided or used by operations. It doesn't matter what the company owes or is owed, just how much cash operations provided. This is a much harder number to manipulate than earnings for two reasons. First, **cash flow**, which also includes **investing cash flow** and **financing cash flow**, has to reconcile with the cash on the balance sheet. Even the stupidest and most corrupt auditors and accountants won't lie about a public company's cash. You get jail time for that. Second, most ways of tweaking results involve goosing numbers that either don't appear in operating cash flow or reduce it.

You can get Enron's last annual report before the bankruptcy, the one filed as of December 31, 2000, online from the SEC or the company's Web site. Operating cash flow looked good on the surface, increasing from $1.2 billion to $4.8 billion from 1999 to 2000, but you also have to look at the components.

Here is Enron's operating cash flow, from the **operating cash flow** section of its 2000 **cash flow statement**:

Enron's operating cash flow
(amounts in millions)

	2000	1999	1998
Net income	$979	$893	$703
Cumulative effect of accounting changes		131	
Depreciation, depletion, and amortization	855	870	827
Impairment of long-lived assets	326	441	
Deferred income taxes	207	21	87
Gains on sales of non-merchant assets	(146)	(541)	(82)
Changes in components of working capital	1,769	(1,000)	(233)
Net assets from price risk management activities	(763)	(395)	350
Merchant assets & investments:			
Realized gains from sales	(104)	(756)	(628)
Proceeds from sales	1,838	2,217	1,434
Additions and unrealized gains	(1,295)	(827)	(721)
Other operating activities	1,113	174	(97)
Net cash provided operating activities	4,779	1,228	1,640

In **management's discussion and analysis of operations (MD&A)** in the 2000 Annual Report, Enron explained the difference between 1999 and 2000 cash flow: "Net cash provided by operating activities increased $3,551 million in 2000, primarily reflecting decreases in working capital, positive operating results, and a receipt of cash associated with the assumption of a contractual obligation."

Positive operating results? That's net income, which rose by just $86 million. The big contributors were decreases in **working capital**, which improved cash flow by more than $2.7 billion, and "other operating activities," which improved cash flow by nearly $1 billion and must involve that receipt of cash for assuming a contractual obligation.

Unfortunately, all elements of operating cash flow are not created equally. In fact, some improvements in working capital are bad signs. Enron did not itemize its changes in working capital, as most companies do. Working capital means changes in **accounts receivable**, **inventory**, other **current assets**, **accounts payable**, and **accrued liabilities**. For example, if a company's accounts receivable rose from $10 million to $12 million over a reporting period, that would reduce operating cash flow by $2 million. If accounts payable, the money the company owes suppliers and vendors, increases from $10 million to $13 million, that would add $3 million to cash flow. Those two components combined would result in a net $1 million increase in cash flow. Keep in mind, however, that a company improving cash flow by not paying its bills (or taxes, for that matter) isn't improving its operations for long.

We can track these changes from Enron's **balance sheet** and figure out what really improved:

From Enron's balance sheet

	2000	1999	Cash flow impact
Net trade receivables	$10,396	3,030	$(7,366)
Other receivables	1,874	518	(1,356)
Inventories	953	598	(355)
Deposits	2,433	81	(2,352)
Other current assets	1,333	535	798
Accounts payable	9,777	2,154	7,623
Other current liabilities	2,178	1,724	454

There was a giant increase in accounts payable, which improved cash flow, but those bills have to be paid someday. Correspondingly, receivables rose by $8.7 billion, more than wiping out the increased payables. That increase in receivables not only hurt cash flow but also suggested that the company was not able to collect its money, or that it might not really be owed that money.

This leaves, among Enron's explanations for improved cash flow, the "receipt of cash associated with the assumption of a contractual obligation." Good luck finding what that means in the financial statements, the footnotes, or the MD&A. But if Enron received cash for assuming a contractual obligation, this doesn't sound like a regular (recurring) operating item. It also appears that if Enron received cash for assuming an obligation, as with the improvement in accounts payable, it just means the bill is going to come due sometime in the future.

If you look at Enron's last quarterly report before its troubles surfaced, filed in August 2001 for the quarter that ended June 30, 2001, cash flow was awful. For six months prior to June 30, 2001, Enron's operating cash flow was *negative* $1.3 billion. Enron didn't even include traditional working capital in this amount, placing changes in receivables, inventories, and payables in a separate category. Including those items, operating cash flow was really negative $2.1 billion for the six months.

Naturally, there was a lot going on with Enron that required further investigation. But you should look at the operating cash flow for every investment. It doesn't take long and can confirm or cast doubt on the earnings numbers and all the summary information thrown at investors that influence their decisions.

The purpose of this book is to get you to read corporate financial statements. You don't have to be a financial genius or a math genius or have X-ray vision. You don't even have to have a lot of time. The reason I call this book *The 5 Minute Investor* is because you should be able to read a financial statement for five minutes and learn more than you ever knew before about a company. Sometimes, five minutes will be enough to convince you to invest, or not invest. Often, you will need to do more work. But if you know what to look for, and what some of that financial mumbo-jumbo means, it will be the best five minutes you spend as an investor.

Because so much of my task is devoted to taking the complexity and confusion (and fear) out of financial statements, I considered it essential that this book be a short, concise explanation of the most important things an investor should learn about a company from its financial statements. I have tried to design each chapter to be read in five minutes. (Maybe sometimes I have assumed you were reading really fast. Take your time, and read the chapters more than once. Some of these concepts might require some extra thinking, but I have tried, wherever possible, to explain the information in the quickest way possible.)

This is the part where I issue my caveats. I am not an accountant or an auditor. I learned my accounting from the School of Hard Knocks as an attorney who frequently had to take depositions of accountants at public companies or their **auditors**. After that, I became a writer on financial subjects, and I have focused on corporate disclosure of financial information. But I can't guarantee that every term is defined the way a CPA or accounting professor would define it, or that I have covered every interpretation of a particular accounting principle or financial transaction. I'm giving you what I consider to be the essentials. That requires simplifying some things and limiting the details on others.

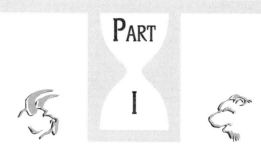

Gimme 5 (Minutes)

Ignore stocks. Think of companies.

If you make your investments based on corporate performance rather than stock performance, you will not only do better over the long term, but you will also focus on more readily available benchmarks. Over the short term, stocks can fluctuate for numerous reasons. Divining those reasons requires a trader's instinct, an insider's access, and a math whiz's understanding of an array of technical indicators. Over time, however, those factors disappear. The only question you should ask yourself is if you want to be a part-owner of this business.

5 Trillion in the Hole:
Why Investors Go Bad

This is the best time ever to be a stock investor, though you wouldn't know it from investor returns over the last few years. Investors are losing fistfuls of money; approximately *$5 trillion* in **market capitalization** disappeared in 2000 and 2001. Enron has everybody fired up about what's wrong with the system, but plenty of stocks took bigger baths than Enron. And for most of those stocks, everyone acts as if it's business as usual.

Gone and, Apparently, Forgotten

	1999-2000 high (per share)	2002 opening price (per share)	Lost market value (in billions)
Cisco Systems	$81.75	$18.44	$460
Microsoft	119.93	66.65	291
Intel	75.81	31.90	288
Lucent Technologies	84.18	6.44	265
Nortel	89.00	7.56	259
JDS Uniphase	153.42	8.70	217
Sun Microsystems	64.65	12.58	166
WorldCom	64.50	14.39	145
Yahoo!	250.06	18.14	132
Enron	90.25	Bankrupt	70

Poor economic conditions contributed to these losses, but less than you think. Some of these corporations were never very profitable, or had terrible cash flow, or didn't have control of their accounts receivable, or weren't bringing in enough money to service their debt, or never had the operations to justify their original market capitalization. Cisco Systems was and is a good company, but it was never worth $550 billion, its peak market capitalization. If you spent a little while reading its financial statements in 1999, 2000, and early 2001, you would have seen the numerous devices propping up results. But few investors looked.

It shouldn't be this way. More investors have better access to more information than ever before. Financial news is everywhere: local and national newspapers, television and cable news, financial networks, and, of course, the Internet. The Internet should be the greatest thing for investors since the **Securities and Exchange Act of 1934**.

Nearly all companies make their financial information available online: **annual** and **quarterly reports**, **proxy statements**, and press releases. Several sites make corporate filings with the SEC available. Business news is reported in real-time on numerous financial Websites. In fact, the financial media have captured the news so completely on the Web that you can find reports on analyst activities, takeover rumors, insider trading, earnings whispers, and unusual trading activity throughout the day.

Unfortunately, distinguishing between helpful and distracting information is difficult. Particularly for the large number of individual investors entering at the tail end of the bull market, few investors have been making good use of all that information. For a little while, investors made money (at least on paper) doing things such as momentum investing, jumping in and out of hot new issues, trading penny stocks, listening to chat-room and message-board rumors, chasing the recommendations of brokerage-firm stock analysts, buying on stock-split rumors, and investing in tech stocks at 100 or 200 times earnings, or dot-coms that had no earnings or realistic business plans.

According to a Committee Report of the **American Institute for Certified Public Accountants (AICPA)**, only 18 percent of individual investors surveyed studied annual reports. Thirty-three percent claimed to "read" them, and 47 percent said they "skim" them. When asked to list the factors they considered "very important" or "somewhat important" to their investment decisions, annual reports ranked sixth among seven information sources.

AICPA Survey Results

"Very Important" or "Somewhat Important" to Investment Decisions	
Their own analysis	87%
Statistical services, such as S&P	83%
Press articles	79%
Radio and television stories	73%
Stockbroker recommendations	70%
Annual reports	66%
Friends and relatives	49%

In another AICPA survey, individual investors put all of the following ahead of company financial statements as information they ranked "extremely important": company reputation, industry outlook, company outlook, the company's stock performance, and recent company developments.

If anything, these surveys, taken just before the Internet took off as a source of investing information, placed corporate financial statements higher than they would become when they had to fight for investors' attention with additional sources such as chat rooms and message boards, financial Websites, earnings estimates, earnings "whispers," and analyst reports.

During this time when investors took their eyes off the ball, companies became much more savvy about how they presented financial information. Except for all those Internet stocks with no earnings, the key corporate event for investors has been the release of "**the earnings number**." This usually meant a per-share number, released quarterly. For nearly all investors, this meant hearing the number announced on CNBC or seeing it on some Website's headline. Few investors even read the accompanying press release, much less the quarterly report filed with the SEC. In a bull market, earnings had to (a) increase, (b) imply future increases, and (c) increase even faster than anticipated.

This put enormous pressure on corporate executives, and they had plenty of motivation to dress up the earnings number as much as possible. This is the age of the superstar CEO. The top executives make salaries like athletes and entertainers, with a gigantic upside in stock compensation. With various **stock options** available to top management these days, it is not unusual for a CEO of a big company to walk away with stock worth hundreds of millions of dollars. (A civil complaint filed in March 2002 by the SEC against Waste Management's former officers claimed that the CEO in the early 1990s used fraud to enrich himself, making $12 million in bonuses and stock options. Times sure have changed. These days, you can't get away with paying only $12 million in severance to a big-time CEO you want to fire.)

Likewise, the stock-heavy compensation of the rest of management and the rank-and-file has translated employee loyalty into an equation dependent on an ever-rising stock price. Pleasing Wall Street has become at least as important as running the business. With no one looking behind the numbers, companies developed sophisticated ways to mask problems and highlight a good earnings number.

Things have to change. The attention focused on Enron in late 2001 and 2002, with its high-flying ways and sudden bankruptcy, has simply reflected the obvious: Companies can endlessly manipulate the earnings number, especially if no one looks deeper into the financial statements. Amid all the finger-pointing—so far, we have blamed paid-off politicians, crooked executives, conflicted accountants, and greedy bankers—no one placed any blame on investors.

This is a mistake. Even though we need a strong regulatory system, and American capital formation needs a level playing field, investors have to do everything possible to protect their money. Your motto should be: "Hope for the best, but prepare for the worst." Even in the worst financial frauds, astute investors can see warning signs. Maybe you won't detect fraud, or see the extent of the problems, but you can see enough to be on the alert. The information I discussed regarding Enron's rotten cash flow wouldn't have tipped you off to its imminent bankruptcy, but it would have told you that the company had fundamental problems that everyone else seemed to be ignoring.

The money you invest should be vitally important to you. It represents your kids' college, your retirement, and your family's security if anything happens to you. You cannot take this responsibility lightly.

The best information available to investors comes right from the horse's mouth, the quarterly and annual reports corporations file with the SEC. The earnings number is just the starting point. There are numerous ways to test the honesty of that number, to determine if it is the result of a good business plan or legerdemain. These reports provide insight into risks and opportunities that can control the company's future destiny. Even a phony-baloney operation leaves tracks behind its manipulations in the financial statement.

But hardly anybody reads financial statements. I have heard all the excuses:

> ➤ "I'm not an insider. I don't have access to what's going on inside a big company. And that's the only way to know what's going to happen."

➤ "I don't have the accounting skills to read financial statements. Who knows what all those numbers mean anyway? And the issuers know every trick
in the book on how to hide the bad stuff or dress it
up."

➤ "Who has the time? I own 10 stocks and am thinking about buying 10 more. These annual and quarterly reports are 20 to 100 pages and are all numbers
and fine print. I can't make reading corporate reports my full-time job."

➤ "What good would it do? If a company is cooking
the books, it is fooling the SEC, some of its own
lawyers and accountants, mutual fund operators,
and money managers. How could I outthink that
army of professionals?"

This book is called *The 5 Minute Investor* for a reason.
Knowledge is power. All the information you need is hiding in
plain view. Five minutes spent reading a company's financial
statements will teach you more than any other source. Sometimes, it comes right out and tells you its risks and problems;
it figures no one is listening. Other times, when companies
are trickier, you have to be more vigilant. But that requires
only that you understand their business story and can compare
certain numbers in the financial statements, between years,
between companies, or between different parts of the same
statement.

Just give five minutes to reading a financial statement after
I help you demystify the process. You will understand your
investments as never before.

Trust a Kennedy:
How We Got This System

2

The first step in understanding financial statements is knowing where they came from. Although companies have been recording their assets and liabilities, and their profits and losses, for owners since time immemorial, the modern system of corporate disclosure goes back to the formation of the original rules for regulating the behavior of public corporations. Congress developed the modern securities laws in response to investor sentiment following the stock market crash of 1929. So many forms of manipulation contributed to the crash that the public lost confidence in the public securities markets. This made capital formation nearly impossible, plunging the country into a deeper and longer depression.

The Securities Act of 1933 and **the Securities and Exchange Act of 1934** established that the federal government would regulate the securities markets. After making a few pronouncements about how broadly these laws applied and going on the record as being against fraud and manipulation, Congress left the business of actually doing something to the newly created **Securities and Exchange Commission (SEC).**

The 1933 and 1934 acts provided the principles for regulating the markets. Issuers of securities must provide certain information to investors, including how their businesses are performing, their financial condition, and the risks of investment.

Companies have to continue providing that information on a quarterly and annual basis. Combined with rules on the conduct of market participants, a regular flow of corporate information would demonstrate that investment in stocks and bonds was a fair game, encouraging the availability of capital and liquidity of investment.

The adoption of these laws involved the kind of grandstanding typical of when Congress decides—always too late—to regulate the financial markets. The likelihood that something positive would come from this long-winded process didn't seem probable when President Roosevelt appointed Joseph Kennedy as the first chairman of the SEC. The patriarch of the Kennedy clan was a brilliant investor and speculator. He made a fortune during the 1920s, but he was considered a good choice only by those who figured he broke all the rules he was establishing.

Despite this inauspicious start, or, perhaps, because of it, the SEC developed a scheme of federal regulation that, with relatively few changes, still exists 70 years later.

SEC regulations require that companies file financial statements quarterly, with a more detailed report annually. The quarterly report is called **Form 10-Q**, filed 45 days after the quarter. The annual report, called **Form 10-K**, must be filed 90 days after the end of the fiscal year.

SEC's **Regulation S-X** describes the form and content of these reports. The controlling principle of financial statement presentations is that they comport with "**generally accepted accounting principles**" **(GAAP)**. GAAP is a slippery concept; it is not a series of precise rules that you would associate with accountants, but a wide variety of guidelines that leave lots of room for interpretation (as you would associate with lawyers).

The SEC has the authority to establish accounting rules, but has generally left that to the accounting profession. From 1936 to 1973, part of the accounting community's professional organization, the **American Institute of Certified Public Accountants**

(**AICPA**), made the rules. Since 1973, the seven-member **Financial Accounting Standards Board (FASB)** has established GAAP. Although the FASB prides itself on being independent of all other business and professional organizations, in early 2002, two of its seven members were former Arthur Andersen partners, and a third used to work at KPMG, another of the giant accounting firms.

Confusing? Don't worry about it. You should be familiar with the names of these organizations because they control the rules. Trying to slog through the rules and guidance of all these organizations is time-consuming and mostly fruitless. Definitely not *5 Minute Investor* work. The most reasonable way for you to improve your investing knowledge is to take financial statements as they are. If you can figure them out and the story makes sense, invest. If you can figure them out and the story doesn't make sense, or you can't figure out what the story is, then stay away. But it is a good use of your time to keep current with the controversies involving financial reporting. If yesterday's scandal does not make tomorrow's rules, it better make tomorrow's investor wary of being burned by the same practices.

Auditing Companies

The **auditor** is the outside professional responsible for reviewing the company's financial statements and determining if they are presented in a manner consistent with GAAP. Auditors are supposed to be independent of company management, but they aren't. Ideally, the auditor works for the board of directors, which represents shareholders and oversees management. Under current standards of corporate governance, however, few boards of directors act as adversaries of management, keeping it in check. In nearly all large companies, the leader of management, the CEO, is also the chairman of the board.

The auditors are not gadflies out to win a reputation as protectors of shareholders. In addition to the consulting services the large auditing firms provide to the companies they audit, the audit work itself is incredibly lucrative, and auditors have to win and keep that business. This is hardly the environment for a critical ombudsman. Although auditors charge the big companies millions of dollars, and a big-time audit can involve armies of accountants working for months—audits have to be done within 90 days of the end of the fiscal year, because the Form 10-K requires audited financial statements—they do not issue a report or commentary on the financial statement. They provide an **audit letter**, which recites that the company's books are presented in a manner consistent with GAAP. In the incredibly rare circumstance where they conclude this is not the case, all hell breaks loose and the company's stock goes down the drain the instant this occurs. With just five accounting firms handling 99 percent of all *Fortune 500* company audits, they tend to resign quietly rather than rock the boat, although all hell usually breaks loose when this happens, too.

Spin

For each form of SEC-required report, companies also release a public-relations version. They send their shareholders, and generally make available on their Websites, their **annual reports**. Annual reports contain a lot of glossy pictures that highlight not just the corporation's business but the attractiveness and ethnic diversity of its workforce. The CEO writes a letter to shareholders proclaiming the previous year as being a "record year" (if the results are good) or a "challenging year" (if they aren't). The report describes the company's business in detail. Finally, at the back, are the financial statements and the fine-print explanations. These are the meat of the Form 10-K, so use this if you want to skip the PR treatment.

To complement the quarterly Form 10-Q, corporations typically present a press release highlighting the financial results, followed by the financial statements. These at least come without pictures, but the more detailed information—additional numbers, descriptive footnotes—is in the Form 10-Q. The SEC does not require audited quarterly financial statements.

Elements

Annual financial statements of public corporations consist of the following elements:

➤ **Management's Discussion and Analysis of Operations (MD&A):** The MD&A provides in narrative form how the company performed during the reporting period. It usually divides the company into operating segments, provides year-over-year comparisons, and provides reasons for changes. You should familiarize yourself with the company enough to know what sorts of comparisons to make on your own to test the strength of the results. You can use this as your background, unless you learn the company's story someplace else. Also, with the attention recently paid to **off-balance-sheet transactions**, **pension income**, and similar hot-button issues, companies are bending over backward to explain those things in the MD&A and the footnotes, figuring if they explain it twice, they can't be accused of hiding it.

➤ **Income Statement:** This is "the Big Kahuna." It describes what the company recognized as revenue, what it recognized as costs, and the size of the profit or loss. The end result (bottom line) is earnings per share (the amount of income earned by the corporation, divided by the number of shares outstanding). Earnings per share gets more attention than all the other information in the financial statements combined. Earnings per share is a helpful number, but it is so easily manipulated that investors need to understand its components as well as understand other numbers in the financial statements.

➤ **Balance Sheet:** This provides the company's financial position, its assets and liabilities, at the end of the reporting period. The assets and liabilities always balance because any difference, positive or negative, is designated as shareholder equity and included as a liability.

➤ **Cash Flow Statement:** This explains how the company's cash position changed from the beginning to the end of the reporting period, taking detours along the way to record net income; **depreciation** and **amortization,** which increase cash flow because they are non-cash charges from net income; changes in **receivables** and **inventory**; and money received or paid from investing and financing activities.

➤ **Changes in Shareholder Equity:** This table is usually of little importance. It explains how shareholder equity changed from the beginning to the end of the reporting period.

➤ **Notes to the Financial Statement:** This is also called the footnotes. This is the very long section of small print that explains all the numbers in the income statement, balance sheet, and cash flow statement. The footnotes will tell you about **revenue recognition** and other accounting policies, acquisitions and divestitures, receivables and inventory, stock options, pensions, off-balance-sheet transactions, and nearly everything else that can affect the quality of results. Don't be afraid. Together, we can make sense of this and you can learn important things about your investments that no one else seems to know.

3

Golden Rules

This is not a conventional investment book. I'm not going to tell you which stocks to buy or sell, or which industries or companies are good or bad. I'm not even going to tell you what to do with your newfound expertise in understanding financial statements.

I feel comfortable letting you figure out these things on your own. There are more qualified authors to tell you those things if you want to hear them. Mostly, however, I hope that taking away your fear of corporate financial statements is enough for one book.

My approach to financial statements, and all corporate activity for that matter, is colored by certain ideas. Most of these are not controversial, but they are not frequently stated. You will make better use of the information in this book if you understand these 10 rules.

Rule #1. The market is efficient, but only in the long run.

When you own a stock, you own a stake in a business. Because investors own such small proportionate stakes, the time it takes for the market to assimilate information, and the different motivations of the market participants, stocks can take on a life of their own in the short run. But in the end, the only way a company can stay in business, much less prosper, is by making enough money to pay its bills and having something left over to pay in dividends, buy back stock, or expand the business to make it better.

Unfortunately, in the short-term, any fool can buy a ticket and take a ride, and investors will constantly be confronted with distractions.

Rule #2. They can hide, but they can't run.

Companies that cut corners and doctor their financial statements, whether using legal or illegal means, eventually have to fess up. The law allows plenty of wiggle room in financial reporting, and law enforcement lacks sufficient resources to go quickly after cheats. Still, if a company claims to be making money, it eventually has to demonstrate it. You can claim fake profits for a long time, but you eventually have to pay debts, loans, or capital expenses, and the people collecting that money are not so easily fooled.

What does this mean for you? First, you will frequently be right but not be proven right for a long time. Wall Street is haunted by the ghosts of short-sellers who were right but went out of business before the truth came out. (Short-selling is the practice of selling a stock you don't own and later buying it—known as "covering"—at a lower price. The practice is legal, provided the brokerage firm with which you have an account can borrow the shares you are selling. Short-selling creates certain risks: One, you are liable for paying dividends to the owner from whom you borrowed the stock. Two, if the stock rises, obviously, you lose money. When you make a regular old purchase of a stock, the most you can lose is your investment, if the stock goes to zero. A short-seller, however, can have unlimited losses because a stock could theoretically rise to infinity.) Be very careful using your investing weapons on short-term strategies. Better still, leave such strategies to professionals.

Second, don't suspend your disbelief just because everybody else does. It sometimes takes awhile for the market to catch up to the truth. Internet companies such as eToys and Webvan were not making money, could not make money, and could conceive of no set of circumstances in which they could make money. Yet because they and other Internet companies' stock kept rising, plenty of smart investors decided that an ability to make money didn't matter. In the end, it always matters.

Rule #3. Nobody reads anything.

During 2002, the fallout from the Enron scandal led many large companies to volunteer additional disclosure about their operations. They can be magnanimous because the current financial information intimidates most investors, and these additional disclosures will make the reports even longer. Very few investors, and virtually no individual investors, read annual or quarterly reports, or their SEC-filed counterparts, Forms 10-K and 10-Q.

You will automatically have an advantage over this mass of investors. In most cases, the insight will be enough for you to avoid the "surprises" that cause fortunes to evaporate in the stock market.

Rule #4. Everything is relative.

Most of my tips for revealing the secrets of financial statements involve comparing numbers. That could mean comparing different numbers on the income statement, or comparing numbers on the income statement to the balance sheet, or comparing the numbers from one year to another year, or even comparing one company's numbers to another company.

For example, to make sure a growth-oriented company isn't just stealing future sales from itself to make current numbers, or counting a bunch of non-revenue transactions as sales, compare the revenue (on the income statement) to the accounts receivable (on the balance sheet). Are they growing at the same

rate? If not, a faster growing accounts receivable could indicate the company is stretching payment periods or including as
revenues money that it can't collect.

One of the best things you can take from this book is the
relationship between different numbers in financial statements.
Comparisons can help you understand the business and confirm
the quality of the reporting.

Rule #5. There is more than one way for you to make money.

In the previous example, a fast-rising accounts receivable
might not be the sign that a company is playing fast and loose
with the numbers. Nothing is a sure thing, either to make money
or to lose money. In dealing with probabilities, consider staying
away from any company about which you have doubts. There
are always other opportunities. Better to be wrong on the investment you pass up than on the investment you make.

Rule #6. Understand the business.

My advice is geared toward investors who don't have the
time or patience to make a full-time study of corporate financial results. That should not, however, relieve you of the responsibility to keep informed. At least understand the general
business of the company whose financial statements you are
pawing through. The financial statements of AOL Time Warner
will involve different issues and risks than the financial statements of Oracle. The better you understand the business, the
better you can understand the nuances of the numbers.

If you can read more of the financial statements than the
highlights I point out, do it. Those glossy sections at the beginning of the annual report and the MD&A can teach you about
the business. You can learn more from the numbers than the
words, but all that information can help you with the numbers.
Take advantage of financial coverage in newspapers, magazines,
television, cable, and on the Internet.

Rule #7. Learn from others' mistakes.

It's bad manners to linger on the road after a really nasty accident, but that does not hold true for investing mistakes. Every time a big scandal is uncovered, news coverage follows. Read it. The more slick maneuvers you understand, the harder you will be to fool. Enron can make you more vigilant about off-balance-sheet transactions, which were, to some degree, disclosed in the financial statements. Lucent can teach you about spotting growth spurred by improperly extending credit. This book will use numerous examples from recent corporate financial statements that fooled most investors, or pose the potential to do so. The more of these you study, the more you understand for the future. Every fraud or catastrophe has its own wrinkle, but they all bend or break the same rules.

Similarly, you can benefit from the investigative work of others. For example, before MicroStrategy announced in March 2000 that it was restating two years of results—restatements that drastically changed the perception of the business—several commentators pointed out flaws in its revenue recognition. Don't necessarily assume such criticisms are true, just as you shouldn't assume everything the corporation says is true. (There is an exception to this: No company that ever blamed short-sellers for the weakness in its stock price ended up as a good investment.) Read about the argument, and then read the financial statements. This should be a requirement if you were a potential investor in MicroStrategy, and a great idea even if you weren't. It's a free lesson in corporate accounting. Take it.

The Appendix provides a list of sources you can read for really great information on financial-statement follies. I wrote this book for investors who wanted a quick, helpful view of corporate financial information, but if the subject interests you, you can do a lot more reading. Certain authors, such as Howard Schilit of the Center for Financial Research and Analysis, and Professors Charles Mulford and Eugene Comiskey of the Georgia Institute of Technology, have been prospecting in these mines for years; they have written excellent books providing other examples of corporate accounting gone bad, different takes on some of the issues we will be covering, and offering more scholarly, in-depth views. Certain business writers, such as Bethany McLean of *Fortune* and Jon Birger at *Money* (just to name two of many examples), provide investors with valuable information whenever they write about corporate accounting or analyze the numbers.

Rule #8. Don't be overly impressed by professionals.

The big mutual funds are good at what they do, and they justifiably get the trust of millions of investors. To the extent you are going it alone, however, don't assume that they know more than you. In fact, there are certain mistakes mutual funds *must* make that you can avoid. First, mutual funds have to be fully invested in their markets. You can sit on the sidelines. Second, once they get really big, there are few investments they can make to generate the returns they need. You, on the other hand, can choose stocks of corporations of any size, in any industry. Third, their benchmark is the **Standard and Poors 500 Index**, also called simply the **S&P**, which is an index based on the market capitalization of 500 large corporations. Therefore, they need a certain amount of their portfolios to include a lot of the big cap stocks, even if that means buying Yahoo at $250 a share. Fourth, their clients like to see hot stocks in the portfolio. If Qualcomm, for example, just quadrupled in price, that might be the worst time to buy it. But mutual fund managers are worried about looking bad for missing it, so they buy it up despite knowing the pitfalls of this kind of investing.

Rule #9. Companies can make more money in only three ways.

A company can make more money in only three ways: selling more, making more per sale, and buying and selling assets at a profit. Picture yourself as the owner of a diner, intent on increasing profits. You can sell more meals (staying open later or advertising better). You can make more per meal (charging more, buying food cheaper, paying employees less). Or you can move assets, selling the whole operation (or some of the equipment) for more than you paid. It is no different for Citigroup or GE or AOL Time Warner.

It is incumbent on you to figure out how a prospective investment intends to make its money, and if its plan works. Far too much attention is paid to tactics that reveal, rather than create, value. A company will not make more money by **splitting its stock**, issuing **tracking stock**, or **spinning off assets**. In the long run, if a company has money in the till at the end of the day (or year or decade), investors will beat a path to its door.

Rule #10. When you buy a stock, you are buying a business.

People forget this, especially during bull markets. Unless you are a short-term trader flipping stocks on market activity, you must remember that you are buying a proportionate share of a business. With a public company, you get less of a voice but more liquidity. Otherwise, $10,000 invested in McDonald's can be compared with $10,000 invested in your friend's hamburger joint. If that amounts to 1/10,000th of 1 percent of McDonald's and 20 percent of your friend's place, line up the financial statements of both and figure out what your proportional share of the results amounts to. If your friend is making more money per $10,000 invested than McDonald's, and it is not otherwise more risky—evaluating things such as liquidity, stability of results, and so on—then you are better off investing in your friend's business.

In the long term, you are buying a stake in the profits, nothing more or less.

4

5 Minutes in the Life of a Company: IBM's 2000 Annual Report

The cover of IBM's 2000 Annual Report promises to tell an adventurous tale: "You're one page away from the no-holds-barred story of one year in the life of a company." It tantalizes you with hints about "big battles, stinging defeats, and gritty comebacks." This is as good a place as any to dig in with a modern, complex corporation's financial statements. Let's see what we can learn in five minutes.

IBM is one of the world's largest and best-known companies, and it is generally regarded as one of the smartest (its motto used to be "Think") and best run. Under Lou Gerstner's leadership, beginning in 1993, IBM fixed its ailing businesses, focused on its best operations, and again became a top American company, increasing earnings every year from 1994 to 2000.

IBM offers some intriguing challenges for investors. It goes out of its way to help investors understand financial reports, providing a detailed guide to understanding financial statements on its Website (*www.ibm.com/investor/financialguide*). On the other hand, it doesn't always get high marks for its own disclosures; it was frequently criticized in the post-Enron environment for using accounting tricks to boost its bottom line. The 2002 IBM controversy developed after it became clear that IBM's fourth-quarter results depended on $300 million ($0.18 per share) from the gain on an asset sale to JDS Uniphase.

Rather than counting the gain as a separate one-time item, IBM took it as a reduction in its **selling, general and administrative expenses** on the income statement. This was not a surprise to investors who spent a few minutes with IBM's 2000 or 1999 annual reports. It did exactly the same thing in 1999, only with a $5 billion deal.

How to get it

IBM's 2000 fiscal year ended December 31, 2000. Therefore, it had to file its Form 10-K with the SEC in 90 days. It also sent a version to its shareholders. (The shareholder version has the great cover and glossy pictures.) IBM, similar to most corporations, makes its financial information available online (*www.ibm.com/investor*). See *www.ibm.com/annualreport/2000* for the 2000 Annual Report. The Form 10-K version is also available online from numerous sources, including *www.sec.gov/edgar.shtml*, *www.edgar-online.com*, *www.freeedgar.com*, *biz.yahoo.com/reports/edgar.html*, *edgarscan.pwcglobal.com/servlets/edgarscan*, and *sec.lp.findlaw.com/edgarindex.html*.

Preliminaries

If you have the time, you should read every word of IBM's annual reports. Our goal for now, however, is just to learn more, and to see if we can do that in five minutes. In the 2000 Annual Report, the financial report begins on page 50. Even then, the three most important parts of the financial statement—income statement, balance sheet, and cash flow statement—don't begin until page 64. If you are looking at the Form 10-K, Part IV, Item 14 contains the financial statements, though IBM simply attached its financial report from the annual report.

Consolidated statement of earnings

This is the income statement. It represents, over the course of the year, the profits and losses of the company.

If you focus solely on earnings per share, IBM is a phenomenal growth story, a behemoth that somehow manages to keep growing. Earnings per share grew from $3.29 in 1998, to $4.12 in 1999, to $4.44 in 2000. These numbers are based on the **diluted shares outstanding**. The difference between the basic and diluted shares outstanding is that diluted shares assume the conversion of all securities convertible into common stock, such as employee stock options. Use the diluted-share number, or at least make sure you are using the same number, if you compare per-share data from different periods.

From IBM's 2000 Consolidated Statement of Earnings (abridged) (in millions except EPS)

	2000	1999	1998
Total revenue	$88,396	$87,548	$81,667
Total cost	55,972	55,619	50,795
Gross profit	32,424	31,929	30,872
Selling, general and admin.	15,639	14,729	16,662
R&D and engineering	5,151	5,273	5,046
Other income	(617)	(557)	(589)
Interest expense	717	727	713
Total expense	20,890	20,172	21,832
Income before income taxes	11,534	11,757	9,040
Provision for income taxes	3,441	4,045	2,712
Net income	8,093	7,712	6,328
Diluted EPS	$4.44	$4.12	$3.29
Basic EPS	$4.58	$4.25	$3.38
Total diluted shares	1,812	1,871	1,920
Total basic shares	1,763	1,808	1,869

Understanding that IBM is considered, although a giant, a growing corporation with a several-year history of improving results and an expectation that will continue, several things in the income statement undercut the conventional wisdom. First, top-line growth was anemic. IBM is a mature business and bottom-line growth is more important, but how long can you grow the bottom line if you don't sell more goods and services? Second, IBM hasn't gone on some giant cost-cutting program. **Selling, general and administrative expense (SG&A)** actually increased by $900 million. (We learn in the footnotes that SG&A didn't actually increase. IBM booked a profitable asset sale in 1999 as a reduction in that year's SG&A.) Third, income before taxes actually dropped slightly in 2000.

So where did the earnings per share increase come from? IBM's provision for income taxes fell by $600 million, which accounts for the entire year-over-year increase. In addition, IBM reduced its outstanding shares by nearly 60 million.

Can these conditions continue? IBM bought back almost as many shares in 2000 as it did in 1999. Companies usually don't buy back their own stock unless they need it to fund employee option plans, in which case the shares outstanding do not decline, or they think the stock is undervalued. On the other hand, companies generally buy back their own stock only if they cannot find a better use for the capital. IBM also spends to fund its operations, but the regular stock buybacks suggest they are bumping up against a practical limit. The reduction in the income tax rate was a consequence of the taxes paid on the sale of the Global Network business in 1999.

Consolidated statement of financial position

IBM's balance sheet (see page 42) shows, at the end of the year, all the company's assets and liabilities. It lost $2 billion in its best assets—cash and marketable securities—and picked up an identical amount in receivables. Short-term debt fell $4 billion and long-term debt rose by a similar amount.

From IBM's 2000 Consolidated Statement of Financial Position
Current Assets (abridged)
(amounts in millions)

	2000	1999
Cash and cash equivalents	$3,563	5,043
Marketable securities	159	788
Notes and accounts receivable	10,447	9,103
Short-term financing receivables	18,705	17,156
Other accounts receivables	1,574	1,359
Total current assets	43,880	43,155

From IBM's 2000 Consolidated Statement of Financial Position
Liabilities (abridged)
(amounts in millions)

	2000	1999
Short-term debt	$10,205	$14,230
Long-term debt	18,371	14,124
Total liabilities	67,725	66,984

Consolidated statement of cash flows

This is IBM's cash flow statement. It allows you to follow the money trail, starting with IBM's earnings, quantifying all its credits and debits (from operations, investing, and financing), ending with the cash on the balance sheet. Cash flow from operating activities was $9.2 billion, but that was down nearly $1 billion from 1999.

IBM's Net Income Versus Operating Cash Flow
(amounts in millions)

	2000	1999	1998
Net Income	$8,093	$7,712	$6,328
Operating cash flow	9,274	10,111	9,273

IBM's net income rose over the three-year period of 1998 to 2000, but the gap between earnings and operating cash flow fell. Non-earnings cash flows were nearly $3 billion in 1998, $2.4 billion in 1999, and just $800 million in 2000.

From IBM's 2000 Consolidated Statement of Cash Flows
Operating Cash Flow (abridged)
(amounts in millions)

	2000	1999	1998
Net Income	$8,093	$7,712	$6,328
Depreciation	4,513	6,159	4,475
Amortization of software	482	426	517
Deferred income taxes	29	(713)	(606)
Gain on disposition of fixed and other assets	(792)	(4,791)	(261)
Other changes that (used)/provided cash:			
Receivables	(4,720)	(1,677)	(2,736)
Inventories	(55)	301	73
Other assets	(643)	(130)	219
Accounts payable	2,245	(3)	362
Other liabilities	122	2,827	902
Net operating cash	9,274	10,111	9,273

Most of the changes in IBM's operating cash flow were negative, and even the positives don't look like recurring items: (1) depreciation, a non-cash charge, fell by $1.5 billion; (2) cash flow received a relative boost because IBM's gains on selling fixed assets (a reduction from operating cash flow) were $4 billion less in 2000 compared to 1999; (3) accounts payable rose $2.2 billion over 1999, but IBM eventually has to pay that money; and (4) receivables rose by more than $3 billion.

You generally expect a healthy corporation to have negative **investing and financing cash flow**, spending money to make money. Even though IBM's core capital spending needs have

been much less than its operating cash flow, the company's
overall cash flow has been negative for three straight years. No
matter how good things look—$8 billion in earnings, $9.2 billion
in operating cash flow—IBM had to borrow money or sell assets
to make it through the year; that was true in 1998 and 1999, too.

From IBM's 2000 Consolidated Statement of Cash Flows Investing and Financing Cash Flow (abridged) (amounts in millions)

	2000	1999	1998
Payments for plant, rental machines, and other property	$(5,616)	$(5,959)	$(6,520)
Purchase of marketable securities and other investments	(1,079)	(3,949)	(4,211)
Proceeds from marketable securities and other investments	1,393	2,616	3,945
Proceeds from sale of the Global Network		4,880	
Net cash used in investing activities	(4,248)	(1,669)	(6,131)
Proceeds from new debt	9,604	6,133	7,567
Payments to settle debt	(7,561)	(7,510)	(5,942)
Short-term (repayments)/borrowings	(1,400)	276	499
Net cash used in financing activities	(6,359)	(8,625)	(4,993)
Net change in cash and cash equivalents	(1,480)	(332)	(1,731)

Negative investing cash flow was $2.6 million worse than
1999, but this was actually a positive development because 1999
investing cash flow received an artificial $4.9 billion boost from
the proceeds of the sale of IBM's Global Network. Financing
cash flow wasn't as negative in 2000 as 1999 but this, too, is the
opposite of what it seems. We know from the balance sheet
that IBM's debt structure changed, but the amount of debt
remained the same. Proceeds from new debt increased by $3.5
billion, but payments to settle debt stayed the same, however,

and repayment of short-term debt rose by just $1.6 billion. Obviously, boosting cash flow by borrowing more money and paying back less is not a good thing for the long term.

Notes to consolidated financial statements

The footnotes to the financial statements are a gold mine of information on the quality of the numbers. IBM's footnotes take up 26 pages of fine print in the annual report. The more time you spend reviewing these footnotes and comparing them to the financial statements, the more you will learn. But if you are pressed for time and have only five minutes, you can still shed light on some of the questions raised in the statements.

A strange and sneaky (but disclosed) practice of IBM is how it accounts for asset sales. IBM, in its "significant accounting policies" footnote, disclosed that it takes those gains and subtracts them from selling, general and administrative expenses: "In addition, general and administrative expense includes recurring other operating items such as gains and losses from sales and disposals of assets other than securities, licensing of intellectual property, amortization or goodwill and currency exchange gains/losses."

In its "acquisitions and divestitures" footnote, the company disclosed that it did this with the big sale of its Global Network to AT&T. "During 1999, the company completed the sale of its Global Network business to AT&T for $4,991 million.... The gain was recorded as a reduction of selling, general and administrative expense in the Consolidated Statement of Earnings."

We could find out a lot more about IBM, but our five minutes are probably up. Before going methodically through the issues that arise in corporate financial statements—addressed in Parts II, III, and IV of this book—let's see what difference a year made for IBM.

5   Another 5 Minutes With IBM: IBM's 2001 Annual Report

The period between IBM's 2000 and 2001 annual reports was tumultuous. IBM had to deal with a global economic slowdown, the effects of the September 11 terrorist attacks, and the succession of popular CEO Lou Gerstner by Sam Palmisano. In addition, after Enron's bankruptcy, IBM was one of the companies singled out as an abuser of the accounting rules. All these matters colored its 2001 Annual Report, which it released in March 2002.

The first section of the MD&A is titled "Road Map," so you can tell IBM has changed its financial presentation. This section points out where the hot-button numbers are and provides "helpful hints."

Consolidated statement of earnings

Even though IBM reported weaker financial results in 2001—lower revenues, net income, and earnings per share—it looks like a stronger company from its financial statements than it did after 2000. Still, you also have to be a bit skeptical about a company that employs so many accounting tricks, even if it is starting to become more up-front about them.

From IBM's 2001 Consolidated Statement of Earnings (abridged)
(in millions except EPS)

	2001	2000	Original 2000
Total revenue	$85,866	$88,396	$88,396
Total cost	54,084	56,342	55,972
Gross profit	31,782	32,054	32,424
Selling, general and admin.	17,197	17,535	15,639
R&D and engineering	5,290	5,374	5,151
Other income	(361)	(1,008)	(617)
Interest expense	238	347	717
Total expense	20,829	20,520	20,890
Income before income taxes	10,953	11,534	11,534
Provision for income taxes	3,230	3,441	3,441
Net income	7,723	8,093	8,093
Diluted EPS	4.35	4.44	4.44

Considering the rotten economy and the way IBM's growth rate looked in 2000, these are not bad operating results. My concern is with IBM's reclassification of some of its expenses from 2000 and 1999. It increased its 2000 SG&A by $1.9 billion and its "other income/(loss)" by nearly $400 million, which makes the 2001 numbers look better by comparison. Always be leery about the future of a company that tries to rewrite its past.

Consolidated statement of financial position

Because of the changes in the income statement, in addition to the fact that we already know we can't believe what appears in IBM's SG&A from one period to the next, the balance sheet and cash flow statement provide a better picture of how the corporation did. The changes in the balance sheet are generally positive.

From IBM's 2001 Consolidated Statement of Financial Position (abridged) (Current Assets, in millions)

	2001	2000
Cash and cash equivalents	$6,330	$3,563
Marketable securities	63	159
Notes and accounts receivable	9,101	10,447
Short-term financing receivables	16,656	18,705
Other accounts receivables	1,261	1,574
Total current assets	42,461	43,880

From IBM's 2001 Consolidated Statement of Financial Position (abridged) (Liabilities, in millions)

	2001	2000
Short-term debt	$11,188	$10,205
Long-term debt	15,963	18,371
Total liabilities	64,699	67,725

When IBM brags about having the flexibility to weather tough times, it means it. Despite a bad economy and a drop in revenue and net income, IBM lowered its receivables by $2.7 billion and inventory by $400 million. Current assets fell only slightly, because cash and equivalents increased by nearly $2.8 billion.

Consolidated statement of cash flows

These improvements in asset quality—more cash, less receivables and inventory—created a dramatic improvement in operating cash flow.

From IBM's 2001 Consolidated Statement of Cash Flows (abridged)
(Operating Cash Flow in millions)

	2001	2000	1999
Net Income	$7,723	$8,093	$7,712
Depreciation	4,195	4,513	6,159
Amortization of software	625	482	426
Deferred income taxes	658	29	(713)
Gain on disposition of fixed and other assets	(317)	(792)	(4,791)
Other changes that (used)/provided cash:			
Receivables	3,284	(4,720)	(1,677)
Inventories	337	(55)	301
Other assets	(545)	(643)	(130)
Accounts payable	(969)	2,245	(3)
Other liabilities	(1,131)	122	2,827
Net operating cash	14,265	9,274	10,111

This appears to be a positive development. Although there are some classification issues you should always look for in the cash flow statement, you generally can't fake good cash flow.

In effect, IBM is shrinking: lowering receivables, selling assets on favorable terms, paying off debt, increasing cash, reducing inventory, buying back shares. That's smart management, especially in a bad market. But it raises an important question: What is the company's future? IBM isn't exactly winding down operations, but every positive thing it accomplished in 2001 had that kind of effect.

The rest

Although the annual report described IBM's finances as of December 31, 2001, the presentation very much reflected the early-2002 concerns about IBM's finances and its history of disclosure. The growing mess inside IBM's SG&A was disclosed better and, to some degree, repaired. (I say "to some degree" because I don't think we investors should let companies off the hook for reclassifying their results to make the present look better in comparison to a suddenly not-so-good past.) Remember how the footnotes explained in 2000 that IBM's accounting policy was to include, as a reduction to SG&A, gains on asset sales? The definition of the same item in the first footnote in the 2001 report does not say that; the first footnote also has a "reclassifications" section that explained the change. In addition, the MD&A on "expenses and other income" described the reclassification of SG&A expenses. Of course, it did this during a year in which it had no asset sales, so under the old formulation, it would have appeared that SG&A skyrocketed. As a percentage of revenue, SG&A was 20 percent of revenues in 2001 and restated to 19.8 percent of revenues in 2000. IBM does, however, still include some unconventional items in SG&A: **bad debt expense,** which most corporations include in the income statement along with the receivables or as a footnote with the income statement specified as "net receivables," and amortization of intangible assets.

IBM also provided, in much greater detail, the financial impacts of its giant pension and retirement funds. IBM treats its pension and retirement obligations as expenses, as it should. It's part of the cost of hiring and retaining employees. Companies have to put aside money each year to fund their pension plans unless, based on a variety of actuarial assumptions (such as how many retirees it will have in future years, how long they will live, what amount they will be paid, and how much the company will earn on the pension assets in the meantime), the plans are overfunded. Because of the great investment markets of the 1990s, IBM and a lot of other companies with big pension-plan assets have not had to spend money on their pension plans. In fact, the return on its already-set-aside assets, which is a combination of actual returns and investment assumptions, has created a large pension surplus. You can't tell from the income statement because the amount of each year's pension earnings are lumped in other income categories, but IBM gets a portion of its earnings from excess of investment gains minus pension benefits. It can't use these earnings because they are in trust for the current and future beneficiaries of the pension plans, but it can impress unwary investors with the gains.

This is all allowed under the accounting rules, but it's sneaky. According to the footnote on retirement-related benefits, IBM's net pension income from its U.S. plan was $1.025 billion in 2001, and $425 million from non-U.S. plans. That accounted for 13 percent of IBM's pretax income. In 2000, total net pension income totaled $1.27 billion, or 11 percent of pretax profits.

IBM also spelled out some other risks and contingencies. In the MD&A, in the section titled "financial condition," it says, "a review of the company's debt and equity should also consider other contractual obligations and commitments, which are disclosed elsewhere in the financial section." Specifically, it referred to lease commitments of $5.7 billion, about $4.3 billion of which are spread over the next five years, and unused lines of credit and other financial commitments totaling $4.5 billion. In the "contingencies and commitments" footnote, it mentioned the financial commitments, which declined about $200 million during 2001.

Once you learn more about these risks, you'll understand the importance of including them in your investment decisions, but they are not particularly dangerous here. Considering IBM's size, its lease commitments do not seem extraordinarily large. The unused lines of credit of customers (and other things such as financial guarantees) are also not out of line. This can be an issue with banks and diversified financial service corporations; they could be lined up as the last to loan money to Enron or

K-Mart or Global Crossing or some other about-to-be-bankrupt corporation that paid the commitment fee in better times. IBM's exposure is limited to such customers because it generally provides financing just for purchases of its products. It is unlikely to be stuck bankrolling the last days of some doomed enterprise.

IBM, despite its sometimes-deserved reputation for ratcheting up results with clever accounting, is not impossible to understand. Every device is disclosed someplace, and it is succumbing to pressure to make more and clearer disclosures, and clean up some of those practices. The important thing is to understand the main components of the numbers in the income statement, balance sheet, and cash flow statement. Then check those numbers against the MD&A and the footnotes to add and subtract the numbers that don't fit with a proper evaluation of the company's operations.

Parts II, III, and IV of this book will go through the main items on financial statements, defining what the numbers mean and the most frequent issues about which you must be aware. Mingled within those sections will be the appropriate MD&A and footnote disclosures that bear on the particular entries in the financial statements. We will conclude by performing an analysis as we just did on IBM on another large, well-known, complex corporation.

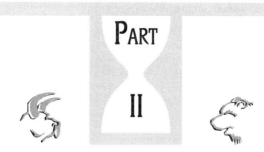

PART

II

The Financial Statement in 5 Minutes

The three components of the financial statement are the income statement, balance sheet, and cash flow statement. Let's get familiar with these documents before we dive into the controversial issues. Once you know what all those line entries mean, you are well on your way to being able to do your own analysis of your investments. Because the text accompanying financial statements—management's discussion and analysis of operations before the statements, and the footnotes after—sheds light on many of these issues, we should also take the time to get comfortable with these as well.

How much time? How much do you think?

The Income Statement in 5 Minutes

6

The income statement describes the company's performance over a quarter or year. It might be called "statement of earnings" or "statement of operations." There is some variety to the presentation, but the income statement generally consists of three categories:

1. Revenues.

2. Costs.

3. Special items.

The end result, which is the number you typically hear in news reports, is earnings per share, which is net income divided by the number of shares outstanding.

Wal-Mart's financial statements are remarkably straightforward. They are short and simple. Wal-Mart probably uses fewer devices to obscure results than any other large company. It also has a great Website for investors, making available its annual reports going all the way back to 1981.

With very few modifications, Wal-Mart's income statement for the year ended January 31, 2001, appears on page 56.

Wal-Mart's 2000 Income Statement
(amounts in millions, except per-share amounts)

Revenues:	
Net sales	$191,329
Other income-net	1,966
Costs and Expenses:	
Cost of sales	150,255
Operating, selling and general and administrative expenses	31,550
Interest Costs:	
Debt	1,095
Capital leases	279
Income Before Income Taxes and Minority Interest	10,116
Provision for Income Taxes	
Current	3,350
Deferred	342
Minority Interest	(129)
Net Income	6,295
Net Income Per Common Share:	$1.41
Average Number of Common Shares	4,465
Diluted Net Income Per Common Share	$1.40
Average Number of Common Shares	4,484

Revenues

Revenues are money a company is due for providing goods and services. If someone orders a cheeseburger at your diner, he gives you three bucks when he's done and you have $3 in revenues. In modern companies, however, revenue recognition is extremely complicated and offers numerous dodges for the enterprising and dishonest alike.

Companies use **accrual accounting**, which recognizes revenues and expenses when incurred, not when settled up. Therefore, once you buy the ingredients, cook 'em up, and hand them over the counter to Wimpy, you recognize $3 in revenue, even though he hasn't begun reaching those short arms into those deep pockets.

Say Wimpy comes into your diner on Thursday and says, "I'll gladly pay you Tuesday for two hamburgers purchased today." If you give him the burgers but don't get the money, you feel poorer, but it still counts as $6 in revenue. In fact, even if you suspect he won't pay, or if Tuesday comes and goes, or the reporting period ends without you being paid, or if you give him more hamburgers without being paid, there are circumstances in which you can still count it as revenue. (Multiply this hypothetical by *one billion* and that's pretty much how Lucent Technologies lost 90 percent of its market value before anybody figured out what was happening.)

For the dishonest, the potential for abuse is unlimited. What if Thursday is the last day of the quarter and Wimpy doesn't come in for his usual burgers? You're $6 shy of your expected revenues for the quarter, so you make him the burgers anyway, leave them in a sack outside the restaurant, and send him a bill. Companies do that all the time and count that as revenue.

What if you're *$6 million* shy of expected revenues? Some companies have put two million burgers in a sack and tried the same scam. Some have even gone so far as to not bother with the burgers and just put bricks in the sack. (Disk-drive manufacturer MiniScribe did this in the late 1980s, eventually going bankrupt.) The dishonesty is eventually revealed, of course, but *you* get caught holding the bag if you invested in this enterprise without being vigilant.

Some companies straddle that line between enterprising and dishonest. If their diner is $600 short on the last day of the quarter, they'll contact Wimpy and ask him to take the burgers on a special deal: He pays full price but he gets two free burgers a week for a year. And they'll also buy that ratty bowler he always wears for $200 next week. HBO & Co., a gigantic health-management company that was later involved in one of the biggest healthcare mergers ever, did this, and its new owner, McKesson, didn't figure it out until afterward. MicroStrategy, an Internet high-flier, went from $333 per share to $4 after it turned out that a lot of its revenues came from deals such as this.

Costs and expenses

Generally, costs are what you subtract from revenues to get income. There are a variety of costs, as well as methods of presenting them on the income statement. You will sometimes see "costs" and "expenses" delineated separately. When that happens, the company is generally trying to distinguish the money necessary to produce goods and services (costs) from the money necessary to sell the corporation's wares, maintain headquarters, and so on (expenses). Companies that separate costs from expenses often include a line called **gross margin**. Gross margin is simply revenues minus costs.

Sometimes, the income statement is very vague on costs and expenses. General Electric, for example, reported "other costs and expenses" for 2000 of more than $30 billion. (This number "fell" to $28 billion in 2001, but it is not particularly easy to figure out why.) For situations such as this, the footnotes to the financial statements provide a wealth of information. Usually, companies will reveal their sleights of hand and weaknesses in the footnotes for the simple reason that no one bothers to read them. As we saw with IBM in Chapters 4 and 5, selling, general and administrative expense was, until recently, where it booked its profits on asset sales, and where it still keeps its bad-debt reserve. Naturally, the heat put on big companies to tell the whole story in the wake of Enron's surprise bankruptcy has increased the amount of information they release, and its readability. Hopefully, this will continue. Even if it doesn't, however, a wary investor can still find the clues.

Unless a company is being deliberately vague, common costs and expenses include selling, general and administrative expenses; marketing; research and development, interest expense; amortization and depreciation; and income taxes.

Selling, general and administrative expenses. Also called SG&A, these include costs associated with sales, running the operation, and maintaining headquarters. Naturally, you want to stay away from companies with high or rising SG&A. As we saw with IBM, you also need to understand what a company includes, doesn't include, or subtracts from SG&A. In IBM's case, it is an almost fruitless exercise trying to decide if it is cutting corporate expenses (as that term is conventionally understood), because its SG&A is a poor proxy for corporate expenses, and it has changed and been restated over the past few years.

Research and development. Although self-explanatory, this can be a sinkhole for abuse. In pharmaceutical and technology corporations, you want to see a big R&D expense. So if a company wastes a bunch of money and can somehow call it research and development, it can turn a negative into a positive, without you knowing.

Interest. This refers to the interest expense on debt.

Amortization and depreciation. When a company incurs significant capital expenses, such as building a plant or buying equipment, it has to spread the expense (both for tax and financial-statement purposes) over the useful life of the expenditure. Because there are many possible approaches for determining amortization and depreciation schedules, a company bent on managing the end numbers has a lot of leeway.

Taxes. Not much can happen here. Like death, nobody has control over taxes. Companies with past losses (also known as **net operating loss**, or **NOL**) can shelter future income. That makes an NOL an asset, to be discussed with balance-sheet issues. Of course, if the corporation is vague about separating operating and transactional gains, that tax amount could fluctuate, as it did with IBM during the period it snuck its asset sales in with operating results.

Special items

There are several items that pop up outside operations on the income statement. Some companies include them (with an explanation) in the results of operations. Others compute net income and then add or subtract these items. Most, in the unaudited quarterly income statements, will designate them outside the **pro forma results** they publicize in the earnings release. These can include **reserves** against revenue, gains or losses on investments, results of accounting changes, **restructuring charges**, accounting for minority interests in joint ventures, gains or losses on **discontinued operations**, and pension gains or losses.

Reserves. Reserves are expenses taken in anticipation of events likely to affect reported results. Remember, despite all the things that can keep a company from getting paid for its goods and services, it can book a transaction as revenue when it finishes its work or delivers the product. The most common reserves are **reserves for doubtful accounts** and **reserves for bad debts**. Any business that sells on credit takes a doubtful accounts reserve on a continual basis; lenders keep a bad debt reserve. As a corollary to revenue recognition, this can be an important measure of a corporation's performance and risks going forward. It is also easy to manipulate.

Investments. Realized gains or losses on investments are one-time items and need to be reported separately, though companies sometimes try to convince investors, through their presentation, to include these one-time, nonoperational events as part of regular earnings. IBM basically says, "We sell assets all the time so it's part of our operations."

Note: Just as when you are ahead in a casino, a company can't count its gains until the investment is concluded (sold). For the most part, the same is true for balance sheet valuation, though there are exceptions.

Accounting changes. There are numerous ways to account for different items. The first footnote to the financial statements usually describes the choices the company has made. If it changes its method, or one of the entities responsible for establishing generally accepted accounting practices changes the acceptable method of accounting for a particular item, the company will note the effect of the changes.

Restructuring (and other one-time) charges. When a company determines that it is reasonably likely that it will incur a one-time cost, it should take the charge at that time, even if the costs themselves aren't incurred immediately. Examples: A company decides to lay off workers or close down operations, or the value of an asset becomes permanently impaired. Wherever there is a lot of discretion, and there is plenty here, there is the possibility for manipulation and abuse. In mid-2001, Cisco Systems took a $2.5 billion loss, writing off the value of certain inventory. By reducing the carrying value of this inventory to zero, there is the possibility that Cisco will be able to, sometime in the future, sell these items and components for something, and call it all profit in some future quarter. These one-time charges are a rare instance in which a company may intentionally make things seem *worse* than they are. Welcome to the concept of **big bath accounting**.

Minority interests. If a company owns a majority interest in a venture (but not 100 percent), it can report all the gains or losses. A separate item accounting for minority interests is supposed to straighten this out. There are issues in financial reporting for the minority owner as well. Berkshire Hathaway, because so many of its assets are tied up in minority stakes in public companies, has developed a number called **look-through earnings** to help investors better understand the performance of its holdings. Minority interests can also be a source of hidden liabilities. This was the main factor leading to Enron's catastrophic fall; It had billions of dollars in obligations in off-balance-sheet limited partnerships, structured to keep their liabilities off the balance sheet. We can find those things if we know where to look.

Discontinued operations. When a company discontinues operations, in addition to any future charges it takes, it has to report the current results, but will, if at all possible, not include them with the operating results.

Pensions. Corporate pension funds constitute a contractual obligation to provide certain benefits. LTV, once one of the nation's largest steel companies, went bankrupt because of its pension liabilities. General Motors has a pension plan that was recently underfunded by $8 billion. General Electric and IBM, on the other hand, have tremendously overfunded pension plans, because the plans' investments have appreciated in the bull market much faster than its expected future obligations. Although they can't access that money, they can claim it as income.

As you can see, there are many traps for unwary investors in the income statement. Nearly all those traps, however, come with clues and warnings, so an investor who knows what to look for can avoid being snared.

The Balance Sheet in 5 Minutes

7

The balance sheet summarizes what a company owns (assets) and what it owes (liabilities) on the last day of the reporting period. The numbers always even out because the difference between assets and liabilities, **shareholder equity** or **capital and surplus**, is included on the liability side of the balance sheet. Shareholder equity isn't some magic valuation. (In other words, *you* are a liability, which may explain why companies treat their shareowners so poorly.) It's just the result of assets minus liabilities. It is almost useless as a measure of a modern company's value. You will rarely invest in a company based on its asset values. You want to evaluate a company's ability to make money, and the balance sheet does not measure that.

The balance sheet is, however, a valuable investing resource. It tells you where the money went, and where it will go. The balance sheet can help you judge the credibility of the story the company communicated in the income statement. In the Introduction, we were trying to judge the quality of Enron's great operating cash flow improvement in 2000. We looked to the balance sheet to see that most of the improvements in working capital, such as not paying its bills, were temporary measures.

The balance sheet also contains some cubbyholes for manufacturing positive results, masking bad results, and storing assets to smooth or burnish future results. We will find and expose these hiding places. The real "balance" on the balance sheet will be between the company's enthusiasm and your skepticism.

Nearly every item on the balance sheet has multiple means of computation. Because you should use the balance sheet as a detective tool and rarely as an independent measure of value, you don't have to consider most of these issues. Obviously, if a company changes to a more favorable valuation, you have to discount the illusory improvement in results. For the most part, however, we will focus on the particular elements of the balance sheet that help us evaluate the income statement. Consequently, most of the discussion on how to use the balance sheet appears in the context of the chapters on the income statement (Chapters 10–22). Chapters 23–29 will summarize those issues as they apply to accounts receivable and inventory (Chapters 23–24) and consider the current brouhaha about off-balance-sheet transactions (Chapters 25–28). Such a discussion could not be complete without an evaluation of Enron's final financial statements (Chapter 29).

Assets

On both the asset and liability sides of the balance sheet, items are listed in declining order of liquidity. For instance, on the asset side, **current assets** generally include those that will be turned into cash during the next 12 months. Current assets include cash and equivalents, marketable securities, accounts receivable, and inventory.

Cash and equivalents. This is pretty straightforward. Valuation issues occur if some of the money is in foreign currencies, but otherwise, even the laziest auditor can confirm the cash balances.

Marketable securities. Because these are current assets, this includes investments expected to be converted into cash within 12 months. "Marketable" also implies that they are fairly liquid. Companies usually value marketable securities at cost or market value, whichever is lower.

Accounts receivable. This is money due from customers. The number is usually "net" accounts receivable, net of the reserve for doubtful accounts. (This is also called the accounts-receivable reserve or the bad-debt reserve.) Because of accrual accounting, companies count the money before they actually receive it. Many forms of financial mischief involve some kind of manipulation of accounts receivable. You must draw together numbers from all over the financial statements (and notes) to evaluate the growth and size of the receivable and the reserve.

Inventory. This includes **raw materials**, **work in progress**, and **finished goods**. Inventory is carried at cost so, presumably, as it moves, the company turns it into cash and accounts receivable (at greater amounts than it was valued as inventory, if the company sells its goods for a profit). On the other hand, growing inventory suggests that products aren't selling.

Because inventory is fluid, there are sometimes valuation issues. If, for example, you retail athletic shoes, you may have, during a particular quarter, bought 1,000 pairs of a certain model, purchased from the manufacturer at different times at prices between $15 and $25. The shoes are all the same, but the manufacturer could have offered them at different prices at different times or depending on the size of the order. If you sell 900 pairs during the reporting period, what is the inventory value of the remaining 100 pairs? The price of the first 100 purchased? The price of the last 100 purchased? Or a blended price based on all the purchases? Companies can choose the valuation method, but they have to disclose it. These methods are called **last-in, first-out (LIFO)**, **first-in, first-out (FIFO)**, and **weighted-average price**, respectively.

Prepaid expenses. This is money paid for future obligations, including rent, insurance, or security deposits.

Investments. These can include securities held by a company that are not marketable or that the company intends to hold for longer than one year. These investments include financial instruments and long-term investments. A large portion of a financial institution's assets is in investments; that's its business. In addition, many companies take financial instruments as payment for long-term contracts and enter into financial arrangements to hedge against risks such as interest-rate or currency fluctuations. Investments in other companies are long-term investments. Berkshire Hathaway, for example, owns a portion of the common stock in Coca-Cola, Gillette, and *The Washington Post*. Usually, investments are marked at cost, although there are exceptions companies will use when it suits them. They do, however, have to disclose when they value long-term or illiquid investments at market value or some value other than cost.

There are numerous valuation issues for such assets. Warren Buffett in particular has complained of how accounting rules require undervaluing Berkshire's investments in other public companies, most of which have appreciated tremendously since it acquired them. Ignore most of this noise. Unless you are investing in a company because of the value of its investments, it doesn't matter. For most companies, these values become relevant only when they start realizing gains or losses on those investments.

Property, plant and equipment (PP&E). These are valued at cost, minus accumulated depreciation. The cost of these items (except land, which does not depreciate) must be spread over their useful life, according to schedules set in the accounting rules. For example, a manufacturing plant built in 1973 for $25 million may require depreciation over 25 years. Every year, the value of the plant on the balance sheet becomes $1 million smaller, until in 1998, when the value becomes zero. There is some discretion in the depreciation schedules, but they are not mirrors of the actual life of items or of market price. After the value on the balance sheet is zero, the plant could still operate for years, or even sell for a substantial amount. Depreciation becomes an expense on the income statement, either as a separate line or as part of the cost of revenue.

By changing the depreciation schedules, a company can manipulate its earnings, because the periodic charge reduces earnings. Waste Management, by doing things such as extending the depreciation schedule on garbage trucks and Dumpsters, inflated earnings by millions per year during the early 1990s. When new management came in, it eventually had to reverse this and other accounting gimmicks, reducing earnings by $1.5 billion.

Intangibles. There is a great deal of controversy about valuation of intangible assets. Coca-Cola's formula, McDonald's golden arches, Mickey Mouse: What are those things worth? Generally, they receive either no value on the balance sheet, or a nominal value, representing the cost of developing them. (Phil Knight, many years ago, paid a copywriter $75 to develop the "swoosh" logo. I bet if you wanted to buy it and put it on a new line of sports drinks, you'd have to pay a lot more than $75.) Unless you are trying to value a company based on its balance sheet—a fruitless exercise when there are better measures available—listen with amusement to this argument from a distance.

One intangible asset attracting a lot of attention is **goodwill**. Definitions of goodwill try to get a handle on its ephemeral value but, like shareholder equity, it is merely a cipher: the cost a company pays to acquire assets in excess of their **tangible asset value**. Tangible asset value is also known as **book value**. Before 2001, mergers could be accounted for in two ways, as **purchases** or **pooling of interests**. In an acquisition, Company A acquires Company B. It records the excess of the purchase price above tangible asset value as goodwill, boosting assets but creating an annual amortization charge against earnings for up to 40 years. Under the pooling method, if the parties could jump through several hoops, the auditors and SEC concluded that no one was acquiring anyone else. It was just two equal parties putting together their assets, so there was no purchase price and no goodwill. The FASB did away with pooling mergers in 2001.

Now, all mergers are acquisitions and the giant goodwill asset always appears. Goodwill is, however, no longer amortized. Annually, companies will review their assets represented by the goodwill on the balance sheet and determine if they have become **impaired**, that is, whether they will earn back their cost within a reasonable time. If those assets have become impaired, the company writes down the asset by the amount of the impairment and takes the charge on the income statement.

During the merger frenzy of the late 1990s, so many large companies changed hands for amounts in excess of tangible asset value that it created two common situations. First, so many companies had their earnings wiped out by these non-cash charges that alternate measures such as **EBITDA** (earnings before interest, taxes, depreciation, and amortization) developed to restate earnings. Second, because balance sheet values have to be written down if they become impaired, the bear market of 2000–2001 has prompted a lot of acquisition-happy companies to declare the value of the acquired assets impaired and take the charge all at once. JDS Uniphase, a dervish of acquisition activity in the late 1990s, the current record-holder, took a $50 million charge to wipe out its bloated goodwill total and, hopefully, the memory of many assets acquired for too much stock. The new rules on goodwill will cause this activity to decrease, especially while companies are reporting sluggish results anyway. AOL Time Warner announced in early 2002 that it would soon take an even larger impairment charge. (It had $128 billion in goodwill on its balance sheet as of December 31, 2001.)

Liabilities

Liabilities are less important to our task. The balance sheet is such a poor instrument for evaluating risks—with the exception of debt, and even that requires us to fill in a lot of blanks ourselves—that you will generally not give it much consideration when evaluating an investment. Usually, by the time a company identifies a risk on the liability side of the balance sheet, it's too late. (We will discuss in Chapter 9 why you are more likely to find out the risks confronting a company in the footnotes than on the liability side of the balance sheet.)

Current liabilities. These include accounts payable, wages, interest payable on debt, rent, utilities, and income tax owed. Similar to current assets, current liabilities concern obligations due during the next 12 months.

Long-term debt. When a company really falls apart, like Enron or K-Mart, the debt is what pushes it over the brink. If you are trying to protect against the downside, shorting a stock, or selling a stock, understanding the debt structure is crucial. The balance sheet and footnotes explain the composition of a company's debt, including amounts, maturities, security, and operating requirements. More often than not, when the Grim Reaper arrives, it is in the form of some covenant the company violated that required it to maintain certain financial ratios. Once violated, the entire loan balance becomes due. If the company has several layers of debt—and most large companies do—each form of debt probably has some clause that says, "If you default on any other debt, this debt also becomes payable in full."

Shareholder equity. This is the number added to (or, in the case of a negative net worth, subtracted from) liabilities to make them balance with assets. This number is rarely meaningful. This number goes by many other names and has various elements, including **book value**, **capital and surplus**, and **retained earnings**.

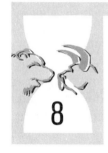

8

The Cash Flow Statement in 5 Minutes

The cash flow statement is your secret weapon. You can pierce most smokescreens that companies throw up to keep you from seeing the true strength of their operations with the cash flow statement. It is nearly impossible to "fake" cash flow. Still, don't completely discard your skepticism. Companies can occasionally get away with classifying some items as cash flow positive when the opposite is true. The organization of the cash flow statement makes discovering these ruses easy. You should never consider a company's earnings as a basis for an investment without looking at the cash flow statement. It's that helpful.

Cash flow refers to the movement of cash in and out of the company over a particular period. The cash flow statement starts with the cash on the balance sheet at the beginning of the period and ends with the cash on balance at the end of the period. The three parts of the cash flow statement are **operating cash flow**, **investing cash flow**, and **financing cash flow**. Each part, and each entry within that part, summarizes where the cash came from and where it went since the end of the previous reporting period.

Ideally, you want to see positive operating cash flow, and cash flow growth that approximates (or exceeds) revenue or earnings growth. Negative investing and financing cash flow are not automatically bad developments; companies generally invest and borrow to fund operations. Generally, negative investing and financing cash flow that exceed positive operating cash flow is a bad sign. In addition, even if a company has positive overall cash flow, some developments revealed in the investing and financing activities of a company could be warning signs.

Cash flow from operations

This starts with net income from the income statement, then adds and subtracts the non-cash items that affected net income and operating items that changed the value of assets and liabilities.

Wal-Mart's fiscal 2000 Operating Cash Flow (abridged) (amounts in millions)

Net Income	$6,295
Adjustments to reconcile net income to net cash provided by operating activities	
Depreciation and amortization	2,868
Increase in accounts receivable	(422)
Increase in inventories	(1,795)
Increase in accounts payable	2,061
Increase in accrued liabilities	11
Deferred income taxes	342
Other	244
Net cash provided by operating activities	9,604

Depreciation and amortization from the period are added to net income. These are periodic charges reflecting the expense and diminution of value of already paid-for assets. The money, however, was already spent (as some previous period's investment), so it doesn't cost the company anything during this period.

Changes in certain assets affect operating cash flow. Rising accounts receivable and inventory reduce cash flow. Increases in receivables can indicate collection difficulties or represent sales achieved with extended credit terms or to uncreditworthy customers. Rising inventory may suggest the company is producing faster than it can sell or is doing a poor job predicting product demand. It can also tip off aging inventory, which may eventually need to be written off. If **accounts payable** (the money the company owes to vendors and suppliers) increases, this increases operating cash flow. Evaluate such an increase with a grain of salt. That money eventually has to be paid, so the positive cash-flow effect is temporary. Likewise, if a company can defer some taxes, that becomes a cash flow benefit of dubious value.

Cash flow from investments

This describes the movement of cash for capital spending, asset purchases and sales, and securities investments. Investing cash flow should be negative for a healthy company. In fact, signs that a company is entering its twilight would be seen in positive investing cash flow; it has stopped investing in its future. The first line, payments for plant, equipment, and other property, is the money the company is spending to improve operations. Companies, obviously, can register investment gains by selling assets or making profitable securities trades.

Wal-Mart's fiscal 2000 Investing Cash Flow (abridged) (amounts in millions)

Payments for property, plant & equipment	$(8,042)
Investments in international operations	(627)
Other investing activities	(45)
Net cash used in investing activities	(8,714)

Cash flow from financing

This includes the cash results of all proceeds of new debt, payment of all debt, stock transactions, and dividends paid. As supplemental information at the bottom of the cash flow statement, companies list the amount of cash paid during the year for income taxes and interest. Because so many income and even balance sheet items are not on a cash basis, the financing cash flow and supplemental items provide a much clearer picture of the company's obligations.

Wal-Mart's fiscal 2000 Financing Cash Flow (abridged) (amounts in millions)

Increase/(decrease) in commercial paper	$(2,022)
Proceeds from issuance of long-term debt	3,778
Purchase of company stock	(193)
Dividends paid	(1,070)
Payment of long-term debt	(1,519)
Payment of capital lease obligations	(173)
Proceeds from issuance of common stock	581
Other financing activities	176
Net cash (used in) financing activities	(442)

Where they try to fool you

Information on the cash flow statement rarely turns out to be inaccurate, even when a company has to restate its financial results. We discussed in the Introduction how Enron tipped its impending immolation in its cash flow statements. In its 2000 Annual Report, Enron reported an apparently robust positive operating cash flow of $4.8 billion. For the first quarter of 2001, operating cash flow sank to minus $464 million. In the second quarter, operating cash flow was even worse, minus $900 million (and even that didn't include some of the items customarily considered as part of operating cash flow). In fact, even its positive operating cash flow for 2000 raised numerous red flags. Almost the entire $4.8 billion came from vague or questionable operating items.

Even though companies can't lie with their cash flow, they still sometimes try to be creative. They sometimes make themselves look better by altering the classification of certain items. You have to be on the lookout for this and simply ignore these attempts.

You should discount any operating cash flow improvements created by stringing along bill collectors (increased accounts payable) or the tax man (increased deferred income taxes). In a similar vein, some companies claim non-operational tax benefits under operating cash flow.

A frequently overlooked item is the tax benefits companies receive for employee exercise of **stock options**. Options are considered an employment expense, and companies get a tax benefit representing the value of the options given to employees. For example, in 2000, Lucent had a $1 billion tax benefit from employee stock options. What this meant was that the exercise of stock options, as a form of compensation, entitled Lucent to claim a deduction in that amount. That's fine, but is it operational? Is it even a continuing benefit for future projections? In fact, heavy and profitable exercise of stock options occurs when a company's stock is surging, which means the company is, indirectly, using its stock performance to bootstrap cash flow. Needless to say, since then, Lucent's employees have been racing for the exits, not to their brokers to exercise stock options.

In some businesses, companies try to classify certain expenses as assets, which affects all three components of the financial statement. For example, a company builds and operates a steel plant. Its main asset is the steel plant, and it is capitalized over its useful life. It sells the plant and starts a software business. Its main asset is the software, so it decides its development cost—something that seems like "research and development," which is generally expensed as incurred—should be capitalized over a longer period than when the costs are incurred, similar to its main asset in the steel business. Most software companies don't subscribe to this logic; Microsoft, which had an annual R&D budget of $4.4 billion for the year that ended June 30, 2001, expenses it all. But a few do. There is nothing crooked about this, as long as it is disclosed. Then it's up to you to notice it.

Likewise, some retail businesses treat their pre-opening costs as assets, capitalized over a longer period than when incurred. Again, the giant in this area, Wal-Mart, expenses such costs as incurred. The rules allow some leeway, so you have to notice when a company capitalizes these costs. This will be discussed further in Chapters 14 and 16. The cash flow statement exposes these practices for you.

If a company expenses these kinds of costs, they don't show up on the cash flow statement. They were expenses against revenues, so the net income number is already reduced to reflect them. If a company treats these gray-area items as assets and capitalizes them, the net income will be increased because the company did not expense the entire item. In the investing cash flow section, there should be an entry reflecting the cost.

The cash flow statement is discussed throughout the chapters on the income statement because it so frequently provides a good measure of evaluating the honesty of the earnings number. Because of this, I devote just one additional chapter to the cash flow statement, Chapter 30, to summarize the lessons from cash flow and remind you of the few ways that companies can tinker with the presentation.

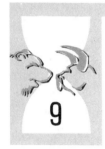

9 The Management Discussion and the Footnotes in 5 Minutes

In addition to the numbers in the financial statements, the text preceding and following the financial statements includes important information. Even if you are trying to do a five-minute evaluation, most modern companies are complicated enough to require you to check the numbers in the financial statements against the text sections. Anything you don't understand will likely be explained in the text. Between the **management discussion and analysis of operations (MD&A)** before the financial statements and the **footnotes** after, companies disclose just about all the risks that should concern investors.

The company is supposed to use the MD&A to explain its results, compare them to prior periods, and describe changes in the business. Management rarely provides more than some murky clues to the risks it wants to hide, but the section summarizes results, points out obvious operating issues, and occasionally overlaps with the footnotes as the place companies place highly valuable, somewhat technical information that it wants to both disclose and hide.

The MD&A also provides some narrative of the company's operations by segment and/or by region. In the post-Enron environment, this is your chance to find out a little more about the parts of the operation. This is where companies such as GE and IBM—large, legitimate enterprises that are nonetheless

under fire for the complexity of their financial information—
are providing more disclosure. GE, in its 2001 Annual Report,
included a detailed explanation of its off-balance-sheet transactions. IBM, in its 2001 Annual Report, provided a lengthy
description of its pension-plan performance, even pointing out
where in the footnotes to find information on the plan's effect
on net income.

The footnotes are more methodical than the MD&A and
are more likely to contain the detailed information missing from
the financial statements themselves. Different businesses, and
even different companies in the same business, may vary the
way they present their footnote information, but the main items
are generally the same. The footnotes in quarterly reports tend
to be much shorter than in the annual report. When reviewing
quarterly reports, look to the most recent annual report for
information about how the company categorizes revenues and
costs, and assets and liabilities.

The substance of those footnotes will be covered in the
appropriate chapters of this book, but the following are the
footnotes on which you should focus.

Significant accounting policies. This footnote contains the
revenue recognition policies, how the company values its inventory, its principles of depreciation and amortization, and
the impact of accounting changes during the year. (This last
item is sometimes a separate footnote.)

Acquisitions and divestitures. Companies summarize the
terms of the assets bought and sold over the previous three
years, with comments and tables on gains, losses, and accounting treatment. For instance, IBM got into hot water with investors in early 2002 when it was discovered that it made its
fourth-quarter 2001 numbers because it treated a sale of assets
to JDS Uniphase as a reduction in selling, general and administrative expenses, giving the impression that the net income
number from the quarter was from operations, free from one-
time events. Regular readers of IBM annual reports know that

IBM has always done it this way (although it's still a sneaky way of giving the impression that operations are stronger than they actually are). IBM said it does this in its description of divestitures in this footnote (it has stopped doing it now that the jig is up). It also described in its definitions section that it considered asset sales as recurring items.

Inventory. Usually, the company will describe how it values its inventory (on a **first-in, first-out (FIFO)** basis, a **last-in, first-out (LIFO)** basis, or otherwise) in the summary of accounting policies. It will break down the inventory total from the balance sheet in a footnote, dividing it into finished goods, work in process, and raw materials.

Receivables. The receivables footnote will provide more detailed information than the line on the balance sheet. Companies that don't mention the reserve on the balance sheet (the receivable number on the balance sheet is usually net of the reserve) include it in the footnote, along with segment or product information, and information about concentration of receivables among particular customers. For certain kinds of receivables, companies keep an ongoing reserve. The footnote provides the size of the reserve, the amounts added to the reserve during the prior period, and the amounts written off. GE's giant finance subsidiary, GE Capital Services, maintains an allowance for losses on financing receivables. You can see by looking at the footnote that the allowance has the potential of turning into a cookie jar for storing earnings when you have them and finding them in slower periods. For fiscal years 1998 to 2001, the size of the allowance increased from $2.7 billion to $4.8 billion. Every year, GE added more to the reserve than it wrote off. This is a nice problem to have—having fewer bad loans outstanding than you thought—but it becomes an investor problem if GE ever starts silently (except for this footnote) reducing the reserve; writing off more in loans than it adds to the reserve, thereby boosting earnings.

Depreciation and amortization. Information on the reduction in value of assets during their useful life, which constitutes a reduction in income but is added back to earnings for cash flow, is provided in several footnotes. The summary of accounting policies may provide the actual schedules. A company will probably provide separate footnotes for depreciation and amortization of big-ticket items such as property, plant, equipment, and goodwill.

Debt. Companies generally discourage you from understanding the debt side of the capital structure. It is a mistake, especially in a weak or uncertain economy, to neglect the amount and composition of a company's debt. The footnote on debt tells you the amount, interest rate, and maturity of all the debt, along with unused lines of credit. Especially for companies in cutting-edge businesses that have not reached their profit potential or those racking up acquisitions, give some consideration to the company's ability to operate if things aren't as rosy as the income statement inevitably makes them appear.

Financial instruments. Sometimes this is called "derivatives and hedging." As the strong dollar of the last decade began to erode the profits of companies doing a great deal of international business, companies started trying to create and trade financial instruments to compensate for these currency risks and losses. Unfortunately, although it is a good idea in theory, it involves some complex transactions that, poorly executed, can create additional risks. It can also convert a stodgy CFO's office into a casino, but without the flashing lights to let anyone know what's going on inside. This led to a series of accounting rules requiring that companies disclose their derivative and hedging transactions.

Other liabilities. Some companies have additional footnotes for liabilities specific to their businesses, such as environmental liabilities. Others simply have a footnote titled "other liabilities."

One-time gains and losses. If a company takes extraordinary charges or profits (from the sale of assets, from writing down or writing off the value of certain assets, from restructuring costs), it may explain the financial impact in its regular footnotes, in a separate footnote, or both. The MD&A will also provide information on one-time events.

Stock options. Stock options can affect corporate results in many ways. Companies can buy back stock to use for the exercise of options, which costs money, especially because companies are selling those shares to employees at a steep discount when employees exercise the options, or it can sell its employees treasury shares, which dilutes existing shareholders. The tax consequences of options can also have a significant effect on the financial statements. Companies set out in the footnotes the amount of options granted, canceled, and exercised during the prior reporting period, as well as the prices at which those options were granted or exercised. The income statement and the footnotes will explain the dilution effect on earnings per share.

Pensions. Reserves and gains based on pension costs and assumptions are contained in a separate footnote. Because pension gains have become a high-profile item, due to their contribution to some big companies' bottom lines, the MD&A section may provide information on pensions. The footnote will include tables on the asset values of the plans, the expected benefits to be paid out, and the assumptions underlying these numbers, along with actual benefits paid and returns over the previous period.

Off-balance-sheet transactions. If the primary responsibility for certain debts is an entity partially owned by an entity other than the company, its liabilities do not appear on the company's balance sheet, even if the company has guaranteed the liabilities or is somehow secondarily liable. Because Enron's collapse was so surprising, and its off-balance-sheet liabilities played such a large role in its bankruptcy, expect some combination of increased voluntary disclosure on the subject and changes in the accounting rules regarding off-balance-sheet transactions. Even under the current system, off-balance-sheet liabilities appear in several places in the footnotes:

1. Sales of receivables, which usually require the seller to assume some liability if the receivables become uncollectible.

2. Lease agreements, which include future liabilities not otherwise appearing on the balance sheets.

3. Pension liabilities.

4. The MD&A discussion of any of these matters.

Segment information. Numerous footnotes will break down numbers in the financial statements by segment. The MD&A will also provide some information on operations by segment. Frequently, companies include a footnote toward the end of the financial statements providing limited financial statement information by segment. If the company does not provide that information to your satisfaction, ask yourself if there could be a reason for this.

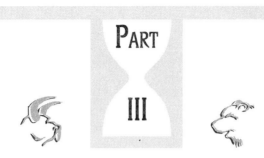

PART

III

The Income Statement

The income statement gets the most attention in this book because it gets the most attention from investors, corporations, and the media. The bottom line, earnings for share, is the most widely disseminated measure of corporate performance. In addition, the earnings number, along with the top line revenue number, is the easiest part of the financial statement to manipulate.

Your best defense is to use the other elements of the financial statement to check the veracity of those numbers in the income statement. This Part will show you how companies manipulate the income statement, and which parts of the cash flow statement and balance sheet can help you combat that manipulation.

Revenue: It's Accrual, Cruel World

10

Revenue, sometimes called **sales**, is the first line on the income statement. Although investors will usually focus on the **bottom-line number**—earnings—the **top line** gets enormous attention. For a growing company, especially a young one, revenue growth implies a level of acceptance of the company's products and services; even without present profits, prospects look good. Mature companies can trim fat, cut expenses, and take advantage of the free marketing that a brand name and established reputation provide, but young companies have to spend to grow. Investors may gauge a growth company's prospects more on revenue growth than present profits.

Of course, investors can sometimes be *too interested* in the top line. Growing revenues without profits is a favorable development only in the short term. Without a business plan designed to turn those sales into profits, you are merely investing in an ever-larger failure. It scarcely requires mention that this was the curse of the dot-com era.

Cash versus accrual

Investors should pay attention to revenue trends, but they also have to evaluate the quality of the numbers reported. Because of **accrual accounting**, a company's true revenues differ significantly from the amount of money in the till, and a lot can happen between when the company records the revenue and the money shows up, if it shows up at all. The guiding principle, under accrual accounting, is that revenues occur when the company has provided the goods or services to create an obligation to pay for them. Likewise, expenses occur when a third party has provided the goods or services to create an obligation by the company to pay for them.

Would things be better under a **cash accounting** system, with revenues recognized when you get money and expenses recognized when you pay them? It would be simpler, but not better. Accrual accounting reflects the real corporate world. Every company is constantly seeking and extending credit. A company might tell you it doesn't allow customers to finance purchases, but unless it ships everything C.O.D., it does. Likewise, it might tell you it has no debt, but unless it pays for everything in advance, it owes money. Companies could abuse a cash accounting system just as easily as an accrual system. Want to cut expenses? Stop paying bills. Boost revenues artificially? Offer deals for customers to pay in advance. We are stuck with accrual accounting, but we can live with it if we understand its wrinkles.

When revenue totals might be fishy

In certain situations, the likelihood that revenues are not as robust as they appear is significant. First, companies doing a lot of acquisitions naturally claim big revenue gains. Determine if the business is growing without the acquisitions or if the company provides segment data, so you can separate different parts of the business. This is one of the few legitimate uses of **pro forma results**.

Second, any company that claims to be a fast grower deserves scrutiny. As a company gets larger, it becomes more difficult, and eventually impossible, to maintain the same growth rates. This means the pressure to perform increases, especially in today's climate where investors build future growth into the stock price and companies are punished if they warn of any kind of slowdown.

Third, companies with revenues coming from only a few customers can fudge significant revenues relatively easily. For Wendy's to fabricate 10 percent of its revenues in a quarter, it has to pretend to move tons of beef to millions of nonexistent customers. For a company with 10 customers, all it has to do is make up another customer.

Fourth, companies that recognize revenue from long-term contracts frequently develop revenue recognition issues. There are many gray areas involving long-term contracts. Some companies try to recognize all the revenue up front. Others follow a percentage-of-completion rule. Still others front-load the revenue but hold back some because of contingencies in the contract. Obviously, the contingencies can drastically alter the amount the company actually collects. For example, Tyco International's home-security business entered into contracts to install and maintain electronic security systems. The SEC, through a **Staff Accounting Bulletin (SAB)**, advised in SAB 101 that revenue should be recognized only when four criteria are met: there is persuasive evidence of an agreement, delivery or rendering of services has occurred, price is fixed or determinable, and collectability is reasonably assured. According to the footnotes to Tyco's 2001 financial statements, "the impact of SAB 101 on total revenue in Fiscal 2001 was a net decrease of $241.1 million...."

Consequently, investors face the risk of making investment decisions based on revenue numbers that include premature or phony revenue. Companies can engage in numerous questionable or phony practices:

➤ Stuffing the channel: Stealing sales from the next quarter at the end of the current reporting period to "make the numbers."

➤ Counting revenues from verbal agreements or other vague, preliminary indications of interest in the company's goods and services.

➤ Shipping unordered products.

➤ Soliciting orders that are impossible to ship before the end of the reporting period or that the customer does not want shipped immediately.

➤ Bill-and-hold sales: Counting revenue from unshipped goods or goods shipped to another company location or warehouse not belonging to the customer.

➤ Signing contracts with side agreements with such favorable terms (such as extended shipping or payment, unlimited rights of return) that the customer is not really obligated to do anything.

➤ Barter transactions dressed up to look like sales.

➤ Up-front recognition of revenue for a long-term arrangement without adequate regard or reserves for contingencies.

Unfortunately, most of these practices are not disclosed in the financial statements. You may not learn the real story until the company can no longer maintain the charade and has to issue poor results or a restatement; or some auditors and officers have to be fired in a search for scapegoats; or the SEC and shareholders have to file lawsuits. There are, however, signals that a company is engaging in such revenue-boosting activities.

➤ **Read the company's revenue recognition policy.** The first footnote to the financial statement is usually a "summary of significant accounting policies." (The annual report tends to include more information than the quarterly reports about accounting policies.) Prior to SAB 101, companies would disclose if they recognized revenue before shipment, or would not specify that they required a written agreement to make shipments or record revenue. AICPA **Statements of Position (SOP)** 97-2 and 98-9 also spell out revenue recognition policies for software contracts. With so many of those questionable activities now clearly out of bounds, those practices have either ceased or gone underground. Still, read the policy. The rules on revenue recognition have a lot of "give" and you can sometimes find out from the footnotes if a company plans to take advantage.

➤ **Compare revenue increases with accounts receivable increases.** Because most questionable revenue recognition policies will not be disclosed, you need to find a proxy on the financial statement for premature or phony revenue. Accounts receivable is your most valuable tool. Rarely will a company cutting corners (or just making up revenues) actually collect on such transactions; if it did, then they would be legitimate. In addition, many revenue-enhancing practices involve longer payment terms or do not create an immediate obligation to pay. Finally, a company hungry for sales may simply give the product to people or entities that don't have the capability to pay for it. All these practices increase accounts receivable on the balance sheet. You can compare the growth rate of revenue and of accounts receivable over successive or comparable periods. You could also figure out how many days of sales are included in the accounts receivable: Divide revenues by 365 for revenue per day and divide accounts receivable by revenue per day.

➤ **Look for signals that the company is under pressure to fudge revenues.** Although you can find some information in the financial statement itself, this is where your understanding of the company is important. Certain companies are prone to overstating revenue: acquisition machines, publicity mills (especially when they constantly issue press releases of deals, associations, or alliances with more established companies, and the terms are vague), and companies run by high-pressure "turnaround experts." With your understanding of the financial statement, you can look at the company's projections and sometimes see that they are patently ridiculous.

All these methods can help you level the playing field when you consider investing in a public company, some of the operations of which are often shielded from your view. Chapters 11–22 demonstrate how a five-minute review of the financial statements could have tipped off investors to some of the most famous restatements and frauds of the past several years.

Revenue Recognition: Lucent

11

As I write this, everyone is scratching their heads and trying to figure out how they got suckered by Enron, which filed the largest ever corporate bankruptcy. In a year and a half, its stock went from $90 per share to $1 per share. Global Crossing's giant bankruptcy would have gotten much more attention if not for Enron. Xerox recently agreed to the largest ever SEC fine (a record that it will no doubt hold for only a little while) and is restating $2 billion in revenues. A few years back, it was Cendant, or Sunbeam, or Boston Chicken, or Waste Management. Whether the practices are called fraud or overly aggressive accounting or obfuscation, the end result is always the same: The investors who bought on the popular wisdom—aping the sentiments of the media, or analysts, or company sound bytes about financial results, or other giddy investors—lost a bundle.

Of course, hindsight is always 20/20, especially when a company is using every device possible to keep the world from finding out the real story. Nevertheless, you can always find traces of the problem in advance, a foreshadowing seen only by those who take the time to look deeper. How much time? Perhaps as little as five minutes.

Lucent Technologies was once the most widely held stock in the United States. Spun off from AT&T in 1996, an impressive growth record from 1996–1999 brought in more than

2 million new investors. They joined the 3 million investors from the spin-off, many of whom had owned AT&T for decades. At its peak in 1999, Lucent had a market capitalization of nearly $300 billion.

Lucent provides telephone equipment, which is a stable, slow-growth business. The increase in competition among service providers and the need to expand and modernize the telecommunications infrastructure led to a growth spurt in 1996 and 1997. We know now, and common sense should have dictated, that this kind of growth can't go on forever. Lucent began cutting corners to force continuing growth in 1998 and 1999. It finally became impossible to sustain even an illusion of growth in late 2000. Lucent's CEO quit; the company started announcing lousy results, restating some prior results; and the SEC investigated its finances. Lucent went from an $80 stock to a $6 stock in 17 months.

If you look at Lucent's income statement, balance sheet, and cash flow statement for 1997, 1998, and 1999, you see two different stories. The income statement shows some flashy revenue and earnings increases. Analysts and the media widely reported these numbers, driving Lucent stock from $20 per share in late 1997 to $84 per share just two years later.

Three numbers represent that success story: revenues, earnings, and earnings per share. (Note that results are through September 30 of each year because that is when Lucent ended its fiscal year.)

From Lucent's Income Statements
(amounts in millions, except per share)

	Original 1997	Revised 1997	Original 1998	Revised 1998	1999
Revenues	$26,360	$27,611	$30,147	$31,806	$38,303
Net income	541	449	970	1,035	4,766
EPS	$0.42	$0.16	$0.74	$0.34	$1.10

Let's ignore for now that Lucent had to restate results in 1997 and 1998, and that it had to restate both years, plus 1999 results, downward in late 2000. Winston Churchill said that history is not kind to countries that keep changing their names; suffice to say, the same is true of companies that keep changing their financial results. Incidentally, this is a common trick. If a company keeps revising its prior results downward, especially if it can do it in ways that don't require formal restatements (making accounting changes, recategorizing items), it can keep making itself look better by comparison with its past. Whenever a company says that it changed prior data to conform to current presentation, take a quick look at the old financial statements and see what it changed. (The exception is when prior per share numbers are adjusted for a subsequent stock split. That was the case with Lucent's 1997 and 1998 per share numbers. The company also restated the revenue and income numbers as well, seemingly redefining its past every time it issued an annual report.)

The balance sheet and the cash flow statement (see page 94) tell a far different story. You can see, with just three numbers on each document, how the glittering results on the income statement were an illusion. Lucent boosted its results by simply giving its product away in exchange for promises of later payment. Selling on credit is, obviously, part of the business, but virtually all the earnings improvement for two years running was the result of a dramatic expansion of credit. Amazingly, as Lucent began extending credit to every Tom, Dick, and Winstar, it lowered its reserve. I'm not talking about just the percentage; it expected fewer total uncollectible receivables off $10 billion than off its previous $7.4 billion total.

With a calculator and just these six lines from the income sheet and balance statement, you can find some disturbing comparisons. In 1997, accounts receivables totaled 20 percent of revenue. The $4 billion in increased revenue between 1997 and 1998 matched a $2 billion increase in accounts receivables. The $6.5 billion revenue increase from 1997 to 1998 coincided with a

$3 billion increase in receivables. Half the increase in revenues came from business on which Lucent wasn't collecting money.

From Lucent's Balance Sheets
(amounts in millions)

	Original 1997	Original 1998	Revised 1998	1999
A/R	$5,373	$6,930	$7,405	$10,438
Reserve	352	390	416	362
Inventory	2,926	3,081	3,279	5,048

Were their customers good for it? In the original 1997 balance sheet, Lucent expected that it would be unable to collect $352 million out of $5.7 billion in gross receivables. (The balance sheet number of $5.3 billion is net of the reserve.) By 1999, gross receivables nearly doubled, to $10.8 billion. The reserve? It barely moved, it went to $362 million.

If you look at just three lines on the cash flow statement, these conclusions are reinforced, and it is clear that accounting changes and fiddling around with receivables and inventory were responsible for almost all the improvement in the company's operating results.

From Lucent's Cash Flow Statements
(amounts in millions)

	Original 1997	Revised 1997	Original 1998	Revised 1998	1999
A/R increase	$389	$484	$1,987	$2,161	$3,183
Operating cash flow	1,946	2,129	1,366	1,860	(276)
Cash at end of period	1,350	1,606	685	1,154	1,816

The better the earnings, the worse Lucent's cash position. Despite apparently outstanding 1998 results, according to the original cash flow statement, operating cash flow went down by $600 million. According to the revision, cash generation still went down, but only by $200 million. Any ambiguity disappears, however, by fiscal 1999. Despite earnings of more than $4 billion, Lucent had *negative* cash flow from operations.

How is this possible? The 1999 cash flow statement, when Lucent was trading at $84 per share and investors couldn't get enough of it, shows the previous three years, including restatements, of cash flows.

Lucent's Operating Cash Flow (abridged) (amounts in millions)

	1999	1998	1997
Net income	$4,766	$1,035	$449
Adjustments to reconcile net income to net cash (used in) provided by operating activities:			
Cumulative effect of accounting change	(1,308)		
Business restructuring reversal	(141)	(100)	(201)
Asset impairment	236		
Depreciation & amortization	1,806	96	(21)
Provision for uncollectibles	75	149	136
Tax benefit from stock options	367	271	88
Deferred income taxes	1,026	56	(21)
Purchased in-process R&D	15	1,683	1,255
Increase in net receivables	(3,183)	(2,161)	(484)
Increase in inventories, contracts in process	(1,612)	(403)	(316)
Increase (decrease) in accounts payable	668	231	(18)
Other operating asset/liability changes	(2,320)	155	(397)
Other adjustments for non-cash items	(840)	(467)	58
Net cash (used in) provided by operating activities	(276)	1,860	2,129

Although earnings rose from $449 million in 1997 to more than $4.7 billion in 1999, by 1999 Lucent was not getting enough money out of its operations to fund them. An accounting change boosted earnings by $1.3 billion without providing Lucent with a dime. The rest of the earnings, and $1.8 billion in depreciation and $1 billion in deferred taxes, both of which reduced earnings, were wiped out by a $3 billion increase in receivables, a $1.6 billion increase in inventories and contracts in progress, and $2.3 billion in other changes in operating assets and liabilities.

The conclusion from all this is that Lucent was a far less healthy company, even at the height of its popularity as an investment, than the earnings numbers indicated. Lucent missed its earnings numbers during the early quarters of 2000. CEO Rich McGinn took the blame, said it was the result of a business segment facing tougher competition than expected, and promised to fix things in a hurry. That explanation bore no resemblance to the truth, though McGinn had great credibility due to Lucent's past performance.

Unless you were on the inside, you wouldn't know for sure that Lucent had been growing by extending credit to start-up telecommunications companies with no real ability to repay Lucent. To get Lucent's customers to keep increasing orders to feed the expectations beast, it also had to steal sales from future quarters, and do it by getting customers to purchase earlier in exchange for Lucent making price and payment concessions.

You wouldn't know these things, but you could smell a rat in McGinn's explanations. Lucent's growth came on the back of selling on credit, and it refused to recognize *any* likelihood of non-payment, raising receivables by $5 billion and reserves for doubtful accounts by a mere $10 million. You would also recognize that, regardless of the reason, Lucent had been losing money on operations, and funding its business through debt, since sometime in 1999.

If you spent a few minutes looking at these things, understanding just the basic concepts and doing simple calculations, you might have avoided being among the 5.5 million shareholders who lost more than $275 billion in the value of their Lucent stock between December 1999 and April 2001.

Revenue Recognition: Sunbeam

12

Sunbeam is a well-known manufacturer of consumer appliances. During 1996, following a few years of declining results, the company brought in new management to restructure the operation. Al Dunlap, nicknamed "Chainsaw" for his hard-charging prowess in turnaround situations—his specialty was cutting employees and operations—led the new management team. Over the next year and a half, Sunbeam used virtually every possible artifice to give investors the illusion of profitability and growth. Many of these tactics involved abuse of restructuring reserves and understating expenses (these devices will be discussed in Chapter 19). Sunbeam also provides a classic study of how a company can fake revenue growth and the signs investors can look for to detect revenue problems.

Sunbeam appeared to execute a stunning turnaround. After years of slow sales declines, Sunbeam shed some businesses in 1997 but still managed to grow revenues by more than 20 percent. The company lost $2.37 per share in 1996, including $337 million in restructuring charges imposed by the new regime; it earned $189 million before taxes in 1997 for net earnings of $1.41 per share. Sunbeam's stock price rose from $12 to $50. Although the first quarter of 1998 was rather slow, Sunbeam was proceeding with three acquisitions and promised that, after additional restructuring and repositioning, profitability and growth would continue.

Instead, in June of 1998, the board kicked out Dunlap and his CFO Russell Kersh. It disclosed that its financial statements for the previous six quarters could not be relied upon, and restatements would be forthcoming. Sunbeam ended up in bankruptcy.

What Sunbeam did

In addition to abusing restructuring reserves and manipulating expenses, Sunbeam tried to pump up revenues to support its story as a viable turnaround. This started in the first quarter of 1997, when it booked $1.5 million in revenue and $400,000 in income from a sale of barbecue grills to a wholesaler just as the quarter was closing. The wholesaler held the merchandise without risk: It could return any merchandise it didn't sell and Sunbeam would even pay the shipping costs. Sunbeam thus began a pattern of achieving its aggressive sales goals with discounts, incentives, and unusually favorable terms. Many of these practices occurred at the end of its reporting periods and stole sales from future quarters or allowed Sunbeam to recognize revenues that would never actually materialize.

In the second quarter, Sunbeam did the same things and began increasing "bill-and-hold" sales. In these transactions, Sunbeam would get a customer to commit to an order but hold the merchandise for shipment at the customer's request. Sunbeam usually offered unusually favorable terms to get these agreements, and it bore all the risks. Customers were never obligated to take delivery or pay until they requested the items.

Sunbeam repeated these practices in the third and fourth quarters. In the fourth quarter alone, bill-and-hold sales accounted for $29 million in sales and $4.5 million in income. Sales to distributors with favorable payment terms and unlimited rights of return accounted for an additional $24.7 million in sales.

Financial results for 1997 looked outstanding. Revenues and net income rose every quarter, for a total of $1.17 billion in revenues, $189 million in pretax earnings from continuing operations, and $109 million in net income.

During the first quarter of 1998, the scheme started to unravel, in the midst of closing three acquisitions and new debt financing. Sunbeam extended the quarter by two days, from March 29 to March 31, to capture $20 million in additional revenues, and it booked $35 million in bill-and-hold sales. Nevertheless, sales still declined to $244 million from $253 million in the year-earlier quarter. Sunbeam lost $0.45 per share, which it blamed primarily on a need for additional restructuring, an unfavorable product mix, and customer decisions to reduce inventory.

What you might have noticed

Investors seemed stunned when Sunbeam revealed the scope of its fraudulent activities. By November 1998, when it issued six quarters of restated results, its stock price had dropped from $52 to $7. Even though Sunbeam designed these activities to be concealed, and investors wouldn't know if a sale included unreasonably favorable returns or constituted an illegitimate bill-and-hold, investors had access to enough information in the financial statements to smell a rat.

The balance sheet. Despite the favorable comparisons between 1996 and 1997 on the income statement, Sunbeam's 1997 balance sheet looked bad.

Sunbeam's Current Assets
(amounts in thousands)

	1997	1996
Cash and equivalents	$52,378	$11,526
Receivables, net	295,550	213,438
Inventories	256,180	162,252
Net assets of discontinued ops. & held for sale		102,847
Deferred income taxes	36,706	93,689
Prepaid expenses and other	17,191	40,111
Total current assets	658,005	624,163

Despite supposedly getting rid of its worst operations, receivables rose from $213 million to $295 million. Inventories rose from $162 million to $256 million. A growing operation should have more receivables and inventory, but Sunbeam was supposedly "refocusing." Sales did increase more than 20 percent, but receivables rose nearly 40 percent, and inventories rose more than 60 percent. Accounts receivable amounted to 79 days of sales in 1996, but 92 days of sales in 1997. This signals potential collection issues and is inconsistent with the story that Sunbeam refocused on its best operations.

Operating cash flow. Despite an earnings turnaround of more than $300 million in 1997, Sunbeam did not generate positive operating cash flow. In fact, its operating cash flow was much better in 1996 before the restructuring. (See operating cash flow report on page 101.)

The $228 million loss from 1996 became cash flow positive after adding back the $154.8 million restructuring charge and $128.8 million in "other non-cash special charges." Sunbeam also had to deduct $43.3 million in restructuring accrual from its positive 1997 results. The increased receivables reduced cash flow by $84.5 million in 1997. The increase in inventory reduced cash flow by another $100 million. Operating cash flow for 1997, in total, was minus $8.2 million.

The footnotes. Unfortunately, the revenue recognition footnote would not be much help. "In limited circumstances, at the customer's request the Company may sell seasonal product on a bill-and-hold basis provided that the goods are completed, packaged and ready for shipment, such goods are segregated and the risks of ownership and legal title have passed to the customer." That is the proper rule, but it was not what Sunbeam was doing. It also disclosed that bill-and-hold sales as of December 29, 1997, were 3 percent of consolidated revenues. This doesn't sound like much, but because the practice accelerated at the end of the year, it amounted to more than $30 million, or approximately 10 percent of fourth-quarter revenues.

Sunbeam's Operating Cash Flow
(amounts in thousands)

	1997	1996	1995
Net earnings (loss)	$109,415	($228,262)	50,511
Adjustments to reconcile net earnings (loss) to net cash provided by (used in) operating activities			
Depreciation & amortization	38,577	47,429	44,174
Restructuring, impairment, and other charges		154,869	
Other non-cash charges		128,800	
Loss on sale of discontinued ops, net of taxes	13,713	32,430	
Deferred income taxes	57,783	(77,828)	25,146
Increase (decrease) in cash from changes in working capital			
Receivables, net	(84,576)	(13,829)	(4,499)
Inventories	(100,810)	(11,651)	(4,874)
Account payable	(1,585)	14,735	9,245
Restructuring accrual	(43,378)		
Prepaid expense and other current assets, liab.	(9,004)	2,737	(8,821)
Income taxes payment	52,844	(21,942)	(18,452)
Payment of other long-term & non-operating liab.	(14,682)	(27,089)	(21,719)
Other, net	(25,546)	13,764	10,805
Net cash provided by (used in) operating activities	(8,249)	14,163	81,516

Footnote 7 to Sunbeam's 1997 Annual Report, Supplemental Financial Statement Data, provides further evidence of the corporation's receivable and inventory problems. Gross receivables rose by more than 30 percent, from $229 million in 1996 to $313 million in 1997. The valuation allowance, however, increased just $1.5 million, from $16 million to $17.5 million. Unless Sunbeam could take on $80 million in new receivables with a reserve of just $1.5 million—a reserve of less than 2 percent, while the prior reserve was approximately 7 percent of receivables—it further goosed revenues by not accounting for bad receivables. The same is true with inventory. It rose from $162 million in 1996 to $256 million in 1997. The largest portion of the increase was in finished goods ($143 million in 1997 versus $85 million in 1996). Sunbeam didn't deal in perishable goods, but raw materials can sit around longer than finished products.

First quarter 1998. Behind Sunbeam's ugly first quarter 1998 income statement were an even uglier balance sheet and cash flow statement. Receivables rose from $295 million to $562 million, and inventory rose from $256 million to $575 million. Comparisons to prior periods are difficult because Sunbeam completed its acquisition of Coleman, the camping-supply company, in March 30, 1998. Coleman's assets and liabilities were included in the balance sheet (a snapshot as of March 31, 1998), but only one day of Coleman's operations were included in the income statement. Because Sunbeam did not break out its balance sheet numbers, there is no way to know how much of the increase was attributable to Coleman.

Coleman's inclusion in the financial statements, however, is something of a red flag. Historically, Sunbeam ended its quarters on the last working day of the calendar quarter. For 1998, this would have been March 29. It acquired Coleman on March 30. Rather than make for the most transparent comparisons possible and keeping that date as the first day of the second quarter, Sunbeam changed the end of its quarter to March 31. This is allowed, but its only possible motive here is obfuscation.

Not only does this maneuver make it impossible to figure out how bad the receivable and inventory problems had become, but it also boosted Sunbeam's revenues by $20 million. Sunbeam mentioned in Footnote 1 of its first quarter Form 10-Q that this increased revenue by "approximately $5 million (excluding the impact of Coleman, which was acquired on March 30)," but it left unsaid that it recorded $15 million in Coleman revenues during those two days. Even though revenues fell by $9 million from the year-earlier quarter, Sunbeam averted the catastrophe of announcing a $30 million revenue decline. This is all allowed under current accounting rules. It's just unbelievably sneaky.

There are two morals to the Sunbeam story: First, reckless or fraudulent accounting can hide a weak business for only so long. Eventually, business pressures—here, customers returning merchandise or refusing to order more and merchandise sitting endlessly in warehouses—force discovery of the bad business and the bad tactics. Second, investors do not have to be geniuses or clairvoyant to figure these things out in advance; they just need to be astute.

13 Revenue Recognition: MicroStrategy

If you are going to invest in technology companies, especially software companies, you have to understand that MicroStrategy's story has happened to hundreds of companies and will continue to happen. Even the SEC can't do much more than shrug at the suggestion that the software business has some inherently dishonest elements.

In its enforcement proceeding against MicroStrategy, the SEC said, "As is common in the software industry, the majority of MicroStrategy's transactions closed in the final days of the fiscal period." Other than a giant scam participated in by everyone in the business, what could explain such a thing? Do people and businesses need more software on the 28th of the month than the 3rd? Do they need it more in March, June, September, and December than in other months?

Maybe it is the collaboration of so many truly brilliant minds that leads these companies to push the boundaries and then cross them. Maybe it is the influence of venture capitalists, who put pressure on these young companies to produce. Or maybe no one really needs software until after the 25th of the month.

In addition to the SEC's SAB 101, the AICPA wrote a statement of position specific to software revenue recognition. Under SOP 97-2, if an arrangement to deliver software does not require significant production, modification, or customization, the company can recognize the revenue up front if the arrangement meets the following four criteria: (1) persuasive evidence of an arrangement, (2) delivery, (3) the fee is fixed or determinable, and (4) collectibility is probable. If the four criteria are not met, or the software requires additional work, the company must apply contract accounting, meaning that revenue must be recognized over the term of the contract. If a contract has multiple elements—software plus later services like support, upgrades, or consulting—a portion of the revenue can be recognized up-front, unless the service component is integral to the software.

MicroStrategy develops and sells data-mining and decision-support software. Revenues have come primarily from software licenses, fees for supporting the software, and consulting. (Increasingly, this is the business model of the software industry—not just selling software but creating a revenue stream by servicing it. Even Microsoft is attempting to develop more of a service business for its products.) MicroStrategy's customers are mostly value-added resellers and original equipment manufacturers, who use MicroStrategy's software as part of their products. In 1998 and 1999, MicroStrategy developed Strategy.com, an information network designed to deliver personalized information through cell phones, fax machines, and e-mail. MicroStrategy contributed the software platform and its partners/customers provided additional content and would market the service.

Even among Internet companies in the "Go-Go Nineties," MicroStrategy was a high-flier. Apart from all the other hallmarks of a successful Internet business—dynamic entrepreneurial leader, cutting-edge business plan, the promise of delivering on the Information Revolution—MicroStrategy had revenues and even profits.

MicroStrategy's 1998 Revenues and Net Income
(amounts in millions)

	1st Q	2nd Q	3rd Q	4th Q	1998 total
Revenue	$19.9	$23.8	$27.0	$35.7	$106.4
Net Income	.542	.942	1.9	2.7	6.1

MicroStrategy extended that streak of success in 1999.

MicroStrategy's 1999 Revenues and Net Income
(amounts in millions)

	1st Q	2nd Q	3rd Q	4th Q	1999 total
Revenue	$35.7	$45.6	$54.5	$69.3	$205.1
Net Income	1.8	3.2	3.8	3.7	12.6

The first quarter represented something of a slowdown from the fourth quarter of 1998, and earnings growth stalled at the end of the year, but it was generally a phenomenal growth story, particularly for an Internet business surrounded by other companies that sported big market valuations without profits or revenues. MicroStrategy looked like it was far, far ahead of the companies created during the Internet Boom.

Investors swarmed the stock. From a split-adjusted IPO price in June 1998 of $6, MicroStrategy's stock tripled in six months. By October 1999, its stock doubled again, to $35 per share. By December 1999, it traded for more than $110 per share. By March 10, 2000, the stock reached its high of $333 per share.

What MicroStrategy did

Contracts after the quarter ended. For a company with such a reliably rising revenue stream, MicroStrategy was dependent on relatively few contracts for a majority of its revenues. During the third quarter of 1999, in which it reported revenue of $54.5 million, a $9 million increase from the previous quarter,

$17.5 million of that amount came from a suspect deal with NCR. Among other problems, the parties did not reach agreement until after the quarter ended. After the end of the fourth quarter of 1999, MicroStrategy signed a deal with Primark, recording $5 million in revenue for the already-concluded quarter. MicroStrategy also announced a deal with Exchange Applications, from which it recognized $14.1 million in revenue for the fourth quarter, a week after the quarter closed. Nearly 30 percent of its revenues for the quarter came from two contracts, both announced after the quarter ended.

Up-front recognition when revenue had to be recognized over an extended period. As MicroStrategy began creating more complex products and developing Strategy.com, it entered into contracts that included substantial additional work. In some instances, the deals were signed before MicroStrategy had actually developed the software. In numerous other transactions, it entered into partnerships to develop and service applications, or agreed to take completed platforms and develop them for new uses. Clearly, under SOP 97-2, the entire amount of the contract could not be recognized up front; the contracts included service components and additional performance on the part of MicroStrategy. In all the deals, in fact, MicroStrategy's future role was so significant that it is unlikely that it could recognize any revenue up front from the agreements. In the fourth quarter of 1998, however, it entered into two multi-element deals, recording the entire $5.5 million in that quarter. At the end of 1999, the $19.1 million in revenue recognized from deals with Primark and Exchange Applications also included substantial, integral service elements, which should have prevented MicroStrategy from recognizing any revenue in that quarter.

Barter and other interested-party transactions to boost revenue. Many of MicroStrategy's heavily publicized deals were more in the nature of joint ventures than revenue-producing contracts. In the NCR deal, for example, NCR agreed to pay $27.5 million to license MicroStrategy software, but

MicroStrategy agreed to pay NCR $11 million in cash for a data warehousing system and $14 million in stock for an NCR unit. The deal with Exchange Applications, likewise, was more than an arm's-length cash transaction. MicroStrategy recognized $14 million in revenue, but it also agreed to pay $4.5 million for Exchange's software. Exchange's initial payment of $30 million consisted of $10 million in cash and $20 million in its own high-flying stock. In a transaction in the third quarter of 1999, MicroStrategy and Sybase swapped some software. Even though this was a barter transaction with no money changing hands, MicroStrategy recognized $5 million in revenue.

On March 20, 2000, just days after PricewaterhouseCoopers signed off on the corporation's 1999 financial statements and shortly before another MicroStrategy stock offering, the company announced that it would have to restate 1998 and 1999 results. It later added 1997 results to the restatement. In total, MicroStrategy admitted that $205 million in revenues during that three-year period should have been $151 million. Net income of $12.6 million was restated as a loss of $33.7 million. Except for the third quarter of 1998, in which it actually restated revenue upwards (from $1.9 million to $2 million), it never had a profitable quarter.

What you might have noticed

MicroStrategy was a publicity mill, issuing press releases, it seemed, every time the CEO wanted to have an audience. To most investors, these deals just fueled their passion for the stock. For those who actually read the releases, they found numerous red flags.

The timing of MicroStrategy's big deals was suspicious. It can't recognize revenue until the deal is signed and the software is shipped. A week after the third and fourth quarters of 1999 closed, it announced three large deals that allowed it to recognize $37.5 million, more than a quarter of revenues recognized during that six-month period. David Raymond of *Forbes* pointed this out in the March 6, 2000, issue, just as MicroStrategy's stock price crossed $300 per share.

The company's revenue recognition policies admitted to the suspicious timing, but its explanation was disingenuous. In the MD&A from second quarter Form 10-Q from 1999, the company said:

> The sales cycle for our products may span nine months or more. Historically, we have recognized a substantial portion of our revenues in the last month of a quarter, with these revenues concentrated in the last two weeks of a quarter. Even minor delays...may have a significant adverse impact on revenues for a particular quarter.... [O]ur quarterly results have varied significantly in the past and are likely to fluctuate significantly in the future.

In the third quarter Form 10-Q, this disclosure disappeared, and then popped up in slightly different form in the risk-factors section. If the contract cycle is nine months or more, why does it always seem to end in the last two weeks of a quarter? If the timing really is a crapshoot, revenue fluctuations should occur. But MicroStrategy's revenues went in just one direction: up, usually 20 to 25 percent per quarter.

In Raymond's *Forbes* article, he asked CEO Michael Saylor about all the last-minute deals. He quoted Saylor as answering, "My job is to manage the business in such a way that nobody's disappointed. I have lots of levers at my disposal."

Likewise, the company's press releases spelled out that these large deals involved MicroStrategy paying for these revenues. The NCR agreement, hailed as being worth $52.5 million, involved NCR paying MicroStrategy $27.5 million to license its software, and MicroStrategy paying NCR $25 million to buy hardware and one of its divisions.

The last thing investors were doing during the dot-com craze was reading financial statements, but the numbers tell the story.

Even though MicroStrategy was one of the few Internet companies making a profit, its balance sheet and operating cash flow statement revealed the usual problems of a company with over-aggressive revenue recognition policies. For the second quarter 1999 Form 10-Q, the balance sheet revealed that MicroStrategy had $46.4 million in accounts receivable, more than 90 days' worth of revenue. Despite $5 million in net income, operating cash flow was minus $632,000. (After the restatement, which lowered revenue by $5 million and income by $8 million, the operating cash flow changed by less than $100,000.) The main culprit was a $14.8 million increase in accounts receivable. For the third quarter, operating cash flow was minus $2.5 million. Net income of $8.8 million was more than offset by a $22.6 million increase in accounts receivable. On the balance sheet, accounts receivable remained at 90 days of revenue.

Millions of investors abandoned common sense chasing hot Internet stocks, and MicroStrategy, even with its misstatements, probably had better operations than most. But if you have to pay a premium simply because a company in a revolutionary industry appears to be "for real," you better make sure it can stand up to the scrutiny of any other public company.

Beat the Check: Methods of Reducing Recognition of Costs and Expenses

14

Just as companies can improve their appearance by counting revenues prematurely, they can achieve the same effect by delaying recognition of expenses. Most of these methods leave behind evidence that a careful investor can find and factor into an analysis of the company's real financial picture. For a few methods that are particularly difficult to detect, you simply have to decide if you want to bet your investment on a company that goes out of its way to obscure its expenses.

There are three things companies do to understate expenses. First, they capitalize certain expenses over a period of years instead of recognizing them as incurred. Second, they take capitalized expenses and extend their amortization period, so the charge against earnings is less per reporting period. Third, they go the opposite way and overstate or prematurely recognize expenses, but they do it as a special charge, hoping shareholders will ignore the item and allow them expense-free revenues in prior or later periods.

Capitalizing versus expensing

When a company spends money, does it count the expenditure as an expense, including it as a cost of revenue during the period incurred, or does it count the expenditure as an asset, amortizing it over a longer period? This is determined by whether the benefits of the expenditure exceed one year. For longer term items, the expenditures are counted as assets and deducted (depreciated) periodically. Items designed to benefit the company over a period of less than a year are expensed as incurred. For most categories, the lines have been clearly drawn. "Property, plant, and equipment" is a long-term item. Research and development, although the benefits are generally over a period of greater than one year, is expensed as incurred by most companies. (Be aware that there are some exceptions.)

The AICPA has tried to clarify some other areas. SOP 93-7, Reporting on Advertising Costs, says that advertising costs should be expensed when incurred, except for narrow exceptions in which the company can meet a high standard of proof, demonstrating and quantifying benefits over a longer period. AOL still tried, several years ago, to capitalize significant marketing expenses. It later stopped and submitted to a settlement with the SEC. Companies still capitalize some advertising. Staples, for instance, capitalizes (over a six-month period) its direct-mail catalogue expenses. Because of the relatively short amortization period and small amount (approximately $20 million out of more than $500 million in total marketing expenses for its 2001 fiscal year), this is usually not a big issue.

SOP 98-5, Reporting on the Costs of Start-Up Activities, concluded that companies should expense virtually all start-up activities. Before this, companies routinely spread out the costs of opening retail stores, restaurants, and hotels.

Chapter 16 provides an example of how you can tell when a company is spreading out expenses it should take all at once. Although the most recent GAAP pronouncements have narrowed this loophole, don't underestimate the ability of financial officers and accountants to find a new wrinkle. Once you see how AOL did it, you will know how to find it if someone else does it in the future.

Stretching amortization schedules

The footnote on significant accounting policies usually includes the company's depreciation and amortization schedules. Unfortunately, in many instances, it will be too broad to be useful. Usually, if a company changes its schedules, it will disclose that in the footnotes. You should be skeptical of any change extending amortization and depreciation schedules.

When the company is really determined to bend the rules, however, it may neglect to disclose it. Chapter 17, focusing on Waste Management's abuse of the accounting rules, which included extending the depreciation schedules of garbage trucks and Dumpsters and included ludicrous salvage values at the end, explains what you can do when the company tries to hide its change to longer depreciation schedules.

Dumping expenses into one-time charges

Chapters 18, 19, and 20 discuss one-time charges of all sorts in detail. These charges go by many names: one-time, extraordinary, restructuring, merger, impairment, discontinued operations, non-operating, non-cash. The most important thing to know about one-time charges is that companies assume investors ignore them and separate them out from results. Categorizing these as non-cash charges encourages ignorance about them. When a company says it is taking a charge to write off assets of $50 million, it is not writing someone a check that day for $50 million. But it did at some time in the past, maybe even borrowing the money to do so, expecting to pay back that loan from the proceeds of what it bought.

When a company realizes it is reasonably likely that it will incur some liability or an asset's value is impaired, the balance sheet has to reflect that discovery. This anachronism from the days when the balance sheet was the most important part of the financial statement has huge impacts on current and, more important, future income statements. If a company is having a bad quarter already, or has just changed management or merged with another company, it has no problem facing its aversion to reporting bad news and taking a large one-time charge.

By the way, the company that plays fast and loose with one of these expense tricks is likely to try out the others. AOL, for instance, after coming up with the bright idea of amortizing the costs of flooding the world with program disks, eventually stretched the amortization schedule for these costs from one year to two years. Because these actions just delayed the inevitable, it finally jumped the chasm by taking all the unamortized costs at once as a $385 million one-time charge, an amount so big that it hoped investors would ignore it and evaluate operations without reference to the charge. Waste Management, likewise, ran the gauntlet of expense-minimizing techniques during most of the 1990s.

A parable about You, Inc.

You figure a certain car will last 10 years and all you can justify in yearly car-purchasing expenses is $2,000, so you buy a $20,000 car. After five years, you sell the car for $5,000. You buy another $20,000 car, figuring it will last 10 years. You sell this one after two years for $12,000. You know for a fact that the cars would have lasted 10 years. You just made a decision to get rid of them.

In seven years, you have spent $23,000 on cars. You buy a third car for $20,000. How much are you going to capitalize every year? If the investors in You, Inc. are as gullible as the investors in publicly traded companies, you can get away with saying $2,000 per year. After all, you depreciated just $14,000 over those seven years. The additional $9,000? Those were *non-cash* charges.

Let's say at some point, you decided what you really need is a monster truck. You convince your spouse only after showing him that you can make enough plowing snow from driveways to pay for it. You borrow $30,000 and get the truck. Three months later, the morning after the first snowstorm, you realize the flaw with your plan: You are lazy and don't like to wake up early. You roll over in bed and say, "Honey, take a non-cash charge of $30,000 for impairment of the truck. I'm going back to sleep." I don't know what your spouse will say in response, now facing a $30,000 debt with no source of repayment, but it probably won't be, "No problem, dear, it's non-cash so it doesn't cost us anything."

The Urge to Merge: Deal-Making and the Financial Statement

15

Before looking at several kinds of expense manipulation, we should discuss the general subject of mergers and acquisitions. Although companies have plenty of tools to obscure their expenses in the absence of deal-making, combining with other companies multiplies the likelihood that the financial statements will be more difficult to understand, particularly with regard to expenses.

The darlings of the last bull market were nearly always acquiring other companies: Tyco International, JDS Uniphase, WorldCom, to name just a few. Even General Electric transformed itself with acquisitions, 993 of them during Jack Welch's 20 years as CEO. A bad stock market exposes a lot of flaws. JDS and WorldCom, stripped of deal-making ability, have stagnated in the telecommunications slowdown. Tyco and, to a lesser extent, GE have aroused suspicion for their accounting in connection with all those deals.

There are three areas in which investors need to understand the impact mergers have on a company's financial statement. First, merging companies accumulate goodwill on their balance sheets, an intangible asset that, when amortized, reduces reported earnings. Second, post-merger results are difficult to evaluate because different periods are no longer comparable.

(A company that keeps swallowing up other businesses always *looks* like it's growing.) Third, companies use restructuring charges to handle one-time expenses following a merger, and those charges are prime locations for obscuring the company's actual operations.

If you understand these principles, you can form your own opinion of the advisability or success of a merger, rather than following the crowd. Chapters 18 and 19 discuss the different kinds of merger-related charges (other than goodwill) that companies take and their impact on the current and future balance sheet and income statement. Chapter 20 discusses the subject of goodwill. Chapter 21 on pro forma and other measures of corporate performance will include how to evaluate pre- and post-merger performance.

Most deals hurt shareholders

Don't assume, like so many investors do, that a company on an acquisition binge is automatically doing a good job. Warren Buffett correctly observed that mergers primarily benefit the shareholders of the target. A study by KPMG of 107 large mergers between 1996 and 1998 concluded that nearly a third of the deals produced no discernable difference in value, and 53 percent actually destroyed value. An update of the study in 2001 showed that 30 percent of the 1997–1999 mergers studied created value, while nearly 40 percent produced no difference and 31 percent destroyed value. The mounting anecdotal evidence agrees. In my first book, *The 50 Best (and Worst) Business Deals of All Time*, I pointed out numerous high-profile examples in which companies did dumb things as part of their acquisition strategies. In Chapter 1 of this book, I listed nine companies that lost much more market value in the last few years than Enron. At least five of these companies were acquisition dervishes: Cisco, Lucent, Nortel, JDS Uniphase, and WorldCom.

Stock and cash are both made of paper

You should also avoid the trap companies set by doing their deals for stock rather than cash. No one seems to worry about the price if it's stock. Stock acquisitions cost you money just the same as cash acquisitions. In fact, they can cost you more, because you (the shareholder), in effect, are the banker. If Corporation A wants to buy Corporation B for $1 billion and wants to borrow the money to pay cash, they have to get a bunch of banks to agree to lend. If everyone is intelligent and does their homework, Corporation B can either earn enough to pay off that loan someday, allowing Corporation A to eventually own those assets free from debt, or Corporation B has enough solid assets to justify lending that kind of money. Banks make some mistakes, but they're not in this business to give away money foolishly. If Corporation A's stock trades at $10 per share and it instead decides to use 100 million shares of stock, it doesn't need a bank; just a copy machine. All it has to do is convince its shareholders, who have a history of voting for just about any deal.

If you pay cash and the new operations are good enough to pay off the debt, Corporation A's earnings and cash flow will rise significantly (although the debt payments will weigh down results for awhile), and you will own the same stake in a more valuable company with more profitable operations. If your company makes the same deal for stock, you will own a smaller share of the larger enterprise, and your company's brilliant judgment (and ability to manage the new enterprise after the merger) is dampened by having to bring Corporation B's share-holders along for the ride.

What if it's a bad deal? If your company borrowed money and paid cash, it has big problems right away. Lots of big bank-ruptcies quickly followed big takeovers in the late 1980s. If your company did this same bad deal but paid in stock, it might do a little better, but not much. It won't have that initial crushing acquisition debt, but your company now has the preexisting debt of both companies and, apparently, not good enough operations to support it. Companies such as Conseco and WorldCom did not go bankrupt immediately after bad deals, but they have barely been surviving.

Remember that when you buy stock, you are buying a proportionate share of the business. If someone issues more stock, your proportionate share declines. It declines similarly if the company has to issue debt (or stock) to make competing claims for your proportionate share of the business.

Goodwill

When two companies merge, the merged entity has to reflect the assets of both companies, at a value based on the price paid. In nearly all instances, the price paid—cash or market value of stock on the day of the stock swap—exceeds the **book value** of the assets acquired. (The price should exceed the value of the assets. After all, if the target company could just sell everything off and get the same value as the merger, why go through the trouble of merging? In addition, control of another company requires a premium in addition to the value of the assets.)

The price paid minus the book value of the assets acquired appears on the balance sheet as goodwill, an intangible asset. Prior to 2001, the FASB required that goodwill be amortized over a period not exceeding 40 years. Although the charge didn't affect the company's cash position—the money or stock already changed hands before the beginning of the amortization—it was a charge against earnings and would lower the reported earnings number that everyone watches so closely. The SEC recognized an exception in situations where the merger was a **pooling of interests** instead of a purchase. Naturally, whenever possible, merging companies tried to classify their union as a pooling of interests to avoid adding goodwill to the balance sheet and, more important, to keep from having to write it down against net income for several decades.

The FASB changed the system during 2001 in two key ways. First, it eliminated pooling mergers. All mergers are now purchases, with goodwill added to the fair value of the merged assets. Second, instead of periodic amortization, companies are required to review the goodwill asset annually to determine if it has been impaired. If so, it performs a valuation analysis and recalculates the value of the acquired assets. Other than this annual review and potential write-down, goodwill acquired through acquisitions is not amortized. This is described in more detail in Chapter 20.

Reserves

Inevitably, when two companies merge, some operations get shut down and some people get fired. After all, if the merger is supposed to make the combined entity leaner and meaner than the separate companies, how can that happen if you keep all the same people and operations? On the other hand, before you follow the masses to hail the new entity, figure the costs associated with such actions when deciding if the merger was a good idea. Investors tend to ignore such "one-time" charges, but if you have to spend a certain amount of money to get the merger benefit, shouldn't you subtract that amount from the benefit? Furthermore, unlike goodwill charges, companies have to spend the money indicated in the restructuring reserve.

You also have to be on the lookout for situations in which a company is using a merger or restructuring reserve to distort its future results, front-loading certain operating expenses so earnings can look bigger in later periods. A company can use this tactic with any reserve; merger charges just allow a particularly good opportunity to make the financial statements look murkier. Manipulating reserves is analyzed in Chapters 18 and 19.

Hidden deals

We have reviewed the financial statements of enough companies to see how they can use asset sales to improve their expense picture. IBM, as we saw in Chapters 4 and 5, sold assets and booked the gains as a reduction in SG&A. You will notice these things if you read the footnotes on accounting polices and acquisitions and divestitures. If a company sells assets, refuses to disclose the numbers, and silently books the sales as reductions in cost on the income statement, you are in a very difficult situation. A company doing this is really ignoring the rules, but it does happen. Waste Management, among its violations of the rules, repeatedly did this during the 1990s. How it accomplished this and how you should deal with it are explained in Chapter 17.

16

"You've Got Expenses!": AOL and Deferred Marketing Expenses

America Online, now part of AOL Time Warner, first became part of the public culture during the mid-1990s, when it inundated us with program disks. We couldn't get our mail or buy a magazine or go through a checkout line without being offered a free trial with AOL. Everybody made fun of it, but that became part of its success.

It cost hundreds of millions of dollars a year to make those disks a ubiquitous presence in our lives. Nevertheless, AOL was able to dramatically expand into this new medium and still appear to be profitable. AOL was never really profitable during this period; it accomplished this by simply not taking all its marketing expenses when incurred. It capitalized rather than expensing those marketing expenses, counting the uncapitalized amount as an asset.

Money spent on advertising and marketing, with few exceptions, is supposed to be expensed as incurred. AOL did not fit into the exceptions, but it failed to include the marketing expense on the income statement anyway. See AOL's income statement from its 1996 Annual Report on page 123.

You see that AOL's marketing expenses are increasing, but they are actually declining as a percentage of revenues. That number, however, represented only the portion of prior-year and current-year expenses amortized during the fiscal year.

AOL's Income Statement, year ended June 30, 1996
(abridged)
(amounts in thousands)

	1996	1995	1994
Revenues	$1,093,854	$394,290	$115,722
Costs & expenses:			
Costs of revenues:	627,372	229,724	69,043
Marketing	212,710	77,064	25,548
Product devel.	53,817	14,263	5,288
General & admin.	110,653	42,700	13,667
Acquired R&D	16,981	50,335	
Amort. of goodwill	7,078	1,653	
Total costs & expenses	1,028,611	415,739	111,546
Net income	29,816	(35,751)	2,154

Not long after AOL started its 1997 fiscal year, as part of a series of accounting and operational changes, it abandoned this practice and began expensing all marketing costs as incurred. In the first quarter, it took a one-time charge of $385 million to write off the marketing costs incurred but not yet taken as an expense. This charge wiped out all AOL's net income from the time it became a public company.

Of course, no one was paying much attention to AOL in 1996. And by the time they did, because it was a frontrunner in the Internet revolution, no one cared that it spent a gigantic amount of revenues to attract customers and wasn't profitable. Nevertheless, in a less heady time or in a more conventional business, the ability to hide expenses can really fool investors.

How would you find out the real story? As is almost always the case, the information is there for investors who know where to look. The first tip-off to this kind of tactic is simply looking at the balance sheet. Whenever a company spends money without deducting it as a cost or expense of doing business, that

money translates into an asset. "Property, plant, and equipment" is the best-known example. That entry constitutes all the
money the company has ever spent on property, plant, and
equipment but not yet amortized.

If you are evaluating a company for investment, look at its
list of assets and see if anything looks strange. The words *unamortized* or *deferred* are usually a hint. AOL had these marketing
costs listed as an asset right there on the balance sheet:

AOL's Balance Sheet, year ended June 30, 1996
(abridged)
(amounts in thousands)

	1996	1995
Total current assets	$270.578	$133,633
Property and equipment at cost, net	101,277	70,919
Other assets:		
Product development costs, net	44,330	18,949
Deferred subscriber acquisition costs, net	314,181	77,229
Other assets	35,878	9,121
Deferred income taxes	135,872	35,627
Goodwill, net	51,691	54,356
Total assets	958,754	405,413

If you need to look further, or the company has included
this kind of expense as "other assets" or in some innocuous-
sounding category, the footnote to the financial statements
describing significant accounting policies will explain what the
company expenses and what it capitalizes. In AOL's 1996 Annual Report, it explained its policy:

> Deferred Subscriber Acquisition Costs—The Company
> expenses the costs of advertising as incurred, except di-
> rect response advertising, which is classified as deferred
> subscriber acquisition costs. Direct response advertising
> consists solely of the costs of marketing programs, which

result in subscriber registrations without further effort required by the Company. These costs, which relate directly to subscriber solicitations, principally include the printing, production and shipping of starter kits and the costs of obtaining qualified prospects by various targeted direct marketing programs and from third parties....

The deferred costs are amortized, beginning the month after such costs are incurred, over a period determined by calculating the ratio of current revenues related to direct response advertising versus the total expected revenues related to this advertising, or twenty-four months, whichever is shorter. All other costs related to the acquisition of subscribers, as well as general marketing costs, are expensed as incurred.

How much did AOL spend during the fiscal year on marketing? When a company's income statement does not reflect an expense, you can usually find it on the cash flow statement. (See page 126.) AOL actually spent $363 million on marketing, not $212 million as appeared on the income statement.

In addition, when you see a big disparity between earnings and cash flow, particularly when the widely reported earnings number is positive and operating cash flow is negative, you should take a closer look to see why the two are so different.

The AICPA has tried to clarify this by stating that advertising expenses should not be capitalized. They also said that start-up costs (such as store, restaurant, or hotel preopening costs) should be expensed as incurred. Still, in the evolving accounting world, always be on the lookout for costs that have not been subtracted on the income statement and that show up as assets on the balance sheet.

AOL's Operating Cash Flow, year ended June 30, 1996 (abridged)
(amounts in thousands)

	1996	1995	1994
Net income (loss)	$29,816	$(35,751)	$2,154
Adjustments to reconcile net income to net cash (used in) provided by operating activities:			
Depreciation and amortization	33,366	12,266	2,822
Amortization of subscriber acquisition costs	126,072	60,924	17,922
Loss on sale of property & equipment	44	37	5
Charge for acquired R&D	16,981	50,335	
Changes in assets & liabilities:			
Trade accounts receivable	(10,435)	(14,373)	(4,266)
Other receivables	(18,293)	(9,086)	(626)
Prepaid expenses & other current assets	(43,305)	(19,635)	(2,873)
Deferred subscriber acquisition costs	(363,024)	(111,761)	(37,424)
Other assets	(26,938)	(6,051)	(2,542)
Trade accounts payable	21,150	60,805	10,224
Accrued personnel costs	12,856	1,850	397
Other accrued expenses & liabilities	104,531	5,747	9,474
Deferred revenue	17,929	7,190	2,322
Deferred income taxes	32,523	14,763	3,832
Net cash (used in) provided by operating activities	(66,727)	17,260	1,421

Waste Management: Dirty Deeds Done for $1.5 Billion

17

Waste Management, before its management purge in 1997 and takeover in 1998 by USA Waste, was practically a lab experiment in creative accounting. (Following the merger, USA Waste took on the Waste Management name.) Considering that Waste was a huge enterprise involved in an essentially profitable occupation—hauling away garbage is an important enough service that, absent pricing pressures, someone has to do it and make a profit—a series of paradoxes developed. First, how could a company play so many games with its books for so long and get away with it? Second, how could a company do so much wrong and still survive?

If there is any aggressive accounting technique that Waste was not accused of having employed, it must be that it considered the idea and rejected it, or tried it so long ago that the statute of limitations has expired. In the SEC's 2001 settlement with Arthur Andersen (Waste's auditor since before it went public in 1971 and the breeding ground for all Waste's CFOs and CAOs until 1997), it found that Andersen, as early as 1988, had been warning the company about its repeated fourth-quarter adjustments to reduce depreciation expenses.

Although Waste Management has been accused of numerous accounting violations over the past two decades—the SEC filed a complaint against its former management in 2002—the biggest focus of its accounting during the 1990s was in the area of understating expenses. As with most accounting tricks, understating expenses forestalls, but cannot prevent, discovery that things are weaker than they appear. (Of course, that is a big enough crime to an investor who buys in during that period.) The particularly insidious aspect to understating expenses, however, is that it can be combined with "one-time" charges, effectively making the bad news disappear forever. If, as is generally the case, investors ignore one-time charges as non-operational matters about the past, a company can habitually understate expenses and then deduct them as a special charge when the day of reckoning approaches.

Waste's business involves a lot of fixed charges. It has to buy garbage trucks, Dumpsters, heavy equipment, and invest in landfill sites. These are all long-term expenditures that appear on the income statement as expenses over the period of the useful lives of the particular assets.

Another thing that made Waste Management an "asset heavy" business was its acquisition policy. During the 1980s and early 1990s, Waste made 100 to 200 acquisitions per year, mostly local waste haulers or other companies in the garbage business. In addition, it developed international businesses, chemical waste businesses, and recycling businesses. In short, it had a lot of business units. Later, when the stream of acquisitions slowed down, it started disposing of units. This included asset sales, spin-offs, **initial public offerings (IPOs)**, and stock swaps with other companies. When some of these spin-offs turned out to be embarrassing failures, Waste Management reacquired them.

In February 1998, Waste Management admitted that it had not been keeping honest accounts for at least the previous five years. (It helped that none of the top officers in 1998 were around during the 1992–1997 period.) It restated earnings for 1992 through 1996 and for the first three quarters of 1997. It took a $3.5 billion pretax charge. Actual net income during those periods, compared with the company's original statements, was as follows:

Waste Management's 1998 Net Income Restatements
(1997 totals are for nine months)
(amounts in millions)

	Original net income	Restated net income	Amount of overstatement
1992	$850.0	$739.7	$110.3
1993	452.8	288.7	164.1
1994	784.4	627.5	156.9
1995	603.9	340.1	263.8
1996	192.1	(39.3)	231.4
1997	417.6	236.4	180.9
Total			1,107.4

In addition, Waste Management diverted $460 million in one-time gains, netting them against unrelated operating costs, allowing it to make that amount of costs disappear. This had no effect on net income, but drastically altered the way operations looked to investors.

Waste Management's violations of the accounting rules should be reviewed in two parts, focusing first on how it delayed recognizing certain expenses, and then how it avoided recognizing them altogether. That second step is the unusual, and more dangerous, practice. Without it, refusing to recognize expenses can't go on for very long; the expenses are there and eventually have to appear. But if you take them all at once as a special charge, investors are encouraged to ignore them as old or irrelevant to the core business; if you net them against non-operating gains, you can continue the charade indefinitely.

Because of the second step, these situations are the most difficult for investors to detect. Even its methods of delaying recognition of expenses discourage close analysis. For example, would you have any idea whether a salvage value of $30,000 for a garbage truck is reasonable or unreasonable? Nevertheless, cutting corners in this fashion does leave a trail. As for the cover-up, you have to avoid investing in companies that engage in these kinds of activities even before you learn why it made its financial situation so difficult to understand.

You should always be skeptical of accounting changes, especially when they increase revenue or decrease expenses. Think about it. Most accounting changes have a negative impact on net income, primarily because the company got strong-armed by its auditor into making the change. How likely is it that an aggressive company would suddenly decide that it had been too conservative in its accounting?

When a company discloses in its significant accounting policies footnote that it is extending amortization periods for certain assets, that's your signal that the company is massaging the numbers. (AOL, in addition to capitalizing some marketing expenses, also increased the amortization period for capitalizing them.) Sure, it will claim to have documentation supporting the charges, and you are not in a position to review that documentation or refute it. Nevertheless, the likelihood that an aggressive company suddenly discovered that its assets lasted longer than it thought, or were worth more than it thought, seems kind of remote, doesn't it?

The problem is that Waste Management did not provide information in the financial statements making it even remotely possible to figure out what was going on. Therefore, your best bet is to follow the rule: "if you can't figure out how they make their money, stay away."

Waste Management didn't disclose when it was changing its amortization and depreciation schedules, or adding to the salvage value. Likewise, when it had non-operating gains like asset sales or insurance settlements, it did not disclose the amounts. It also failed to provide any details on the existence and composition of its reserve accounts for matters like self-insurance and post-closure site remediation.

This is what Waste Management's 1995 income statement looked like, omitting only the lines on per-share information and discontinued operations.

WMX Technologies's (Waste Management) 1995 Income Statement (amounts in thousands)

REVENUE	$10,247,617
Operating Expenses	7,045,070
Special Charges	335,193
Goodwill Amortization	117,482
Selling and Administrative Expenses	1,174,636
Interest Expense	424,736
Interest Income	(39,804)
Minority Interest	94,359
Sundry Income, Net	(75,688)
Income From Continuing Operations Before Income Taxes	1,171,633
Provision For Income Taxes	517,043
Income From Continuing Operations	654,590

A paperboy has a longer income statement than that. Operating expenses of $7 billion and no detail whatsoever? The amount is not broken down in the footnotes, either. If you want to know how much of that $7 billion is depreciation and amortization, you have to look to the cash flow statement. And what about "sundry income"? There isn't more than a line or two in any filing, giving some reference to the disposition of stock or assets without providing amounts or the size or gains or losses.

The company hid its problems on a continuing basis by taking charges and selling assets. According to the SEC, in 1992, Waste Management gained $351 million by selling shares in Waste Management International. It reported only $240 million of the gain "from stock transactions of subsidiaries" on the income statement. It used the remaining $111 million to remove certain past misstatements and current period expenses. Because of its very general presentation of revenues and costs, it could knock $50 million off its expenses and tell you it was keeping costs under control. You'd be none the wiser. The company's income would be the same, but you would think its operations were stronger and more profitable. Waste Management never provided its carrying costs of the assets sold in the IPO so you would never know the correct number.

Waste did this numerous times, selling a subsidiary in 1994 for a $25 million gain, never disclosing the terms of the deal or the carrying cost of the subsidiary, and netting the $25 million against operating expenses. It also did this with half of a $50 million insurance litigation settlement later in 1994. On the last day of 1995, Waste Management swapped its interest in a subsidiary of ServiceMaster for stock in the parent. It gained $160 million on the transaction, but applied the entire amount to reduce operating expenses.

The sheer volume of the "special" charges should spook an investor. One of the main goals of financial presentation is to allow investors to compare corporate performance over time. If the company is always making one-time additions or subtractions, it is keeping you from doing this. Look at all the action in a footnote of Waste's 1993 Annual Report:

> The Company's results of operations for 1991 include a special charge of $296,000,000 before tax and minority interest, primarily to reflect then current estimates of the environmental remediation liabilities.... Results of operations for 1991 also include a pretax gain of approximately $47,000,000 realized by WTI on the sale of its French abrasives business.
>
> Results for 1992 include a non-taxable gain of $240,000,000 (before minority interest) resulting from the initial public offering by WM International....
>
> During the second quarter of 1992, the Company recorded special charges of $159,700,000 before tax and minority interest, primarily related to a writedown of the Company's medical waste business and CWM incinerators in Chicago, Illinois and Tijuana, Mexico....
>
> During the fourth quarter of 1992, the Company recorded a special charge of $60,200,000 before tax and minority interest as a result of charges by Brand and CWM

to reflect a writedown of Brand's investment in its asbestos abatement business and certain restructuring costs....

During the third quarter of 1993, the Company recorded a special charge of $550,000,000 before tax and minority interest as a result of CWM recording a special asset revaluation and restructuring charge. The charge consisted of $381,000,000 to write down assets, primarily incinerators, and $169,000,000 for the probable cash expenditures (the majority of which will be made by the end of 1994 except for closure, post-closure and related costs at facilities closed or to be closed)....

The Company's results for 1993 include a gain of $15,900,000 (before minority interest) related to the issuance of shares by the Company's Rust subsidiary in the second quarter.

You don't need to understand all those charges, or know that some of them were misstated, to see that you can't compare Waste Management's financial statements among reporting periods or understand its expenses or reserves. Your only choice is to put your faith in management.

If you look at the cash flow statements of Waste Management during this period, you would get a better picture of operations. The entries would not have shown the huge gap between Waste's financial presentation and GAAP, but you can see more clearly that the company is flailing around trying to figure out, without success, how to grow. The gap between its original and restated cash flow was much smaller than its net income numbers.

From Waste Management's 1997 Annual Report (amounts in thousands)

	Orig. cash flow	Restated cash flow	Orig. net income	Restated net income
1994	$1,808,237	$1,734,423	$784,381	$627,508
1995	2,035,258	1,948,571	603,899	340,097
1996	1,906,873	1,640,028	192,085	(39,307)

Again, I don't think you could foil this scheme by looking at cash flow; it just provides a clearer view of the business, especially if there is some funny business going on with amortization and depreciation amounts.

It's not exactly *5 Minute Investor* work, but if you pulled Waste Management's quarterly depreciation and amortization expenses, which are lumped into "operating expenses" on the income statement, from cash flow, you can see a static level of charges that doesn't square with the expansion of the company's assets.

Waste Management's Quarterly Depreciation and Amortization Expense (amounts in millions)

	1st Q	2nd Q	3rd Q	4th Q	Total
1993	$194	$205	$187	$210	$796
1994	212	227	221	220	880
1995	213	220	228	224	885
1996	223	239	232	224	920
1997	213	212	224		

Unfortunately, this is not the kind of analysis you can quickly do for all your prospective investments. That you would have to resort to this, however, should be warning enough: If you can't figure it out, pass it up!

If you are going to invest in a company that won't disclose the details of its operations in a coherent way, you have to trust completely the people running the company to take care of you, because you know from the financial statements that you can't take care of yourself. Is there any corporation, especially one that goes out of its way to keep you from figuring out its story, that you can trust that much? Don't fall in love with a corporation; it can't love you back.

Restructuring Charges: The Big Bath That Gets You Dirty

There are exceptions to the rule that the income statement contains only current sales and costs. When a company is reasonably certain of a future loss, or some of its capitalized assets become permanently impaired, it has to adjust the value on the balance sheet and take the loss.

Contrary to usual form, companies embrace these charges and make them as large as possible. Investors tend to ignore one-time events, either considering them "not operational" or looking past them to "operating earnings." And if anyone notices and penalizes the company, it might as well shovel every bit of dirty business into view, to make things cleaner for the future. Hence, such charges are referred to as "**big bath accounting**."

Investors should always be skeptical of special charges. The original idea for asset write-downs was that the balance sheet had to accurately reflect the value of assets. The effect on the income statement—a loss to reflect that diminution in value—was considered secondary. But investors nowadays are (and should be) more concerned with the income statement than the balance sheet, and marking down assets to make balance sheets more accurate, itself a debatable proposition, is making the income statement murkier. In addition, if investors don't pay enough attention to these charges, they are letting companies get away with past mistakes and get a free ride on some future expenses.

Let's say a company has a plant with an unamortized value of $20 million, and it employs 1,000 people. If the company and the plant are successful, it keeps amortizing the plant and recognizing the expense of paying 1,000 employees. A lousy company with a lousy plant decides to shut it down and fire the workers. It is costing shareholders money by running this bad operation, but the special charge wipes the $20 million off the balance sheet, saving the company the yearly depreciation expenses. It paid the same for the plant as the successful company. The salaries, benefits, and severance of the 1,000 employees, expenses a company with good operations has to keep recognizing, become part of the special charge, even if the bad company doesn't close down the plant immediately. A good business, therefore, costs money, but a bad business, once you ignore the special charges, is free.

There is no secret to decoding big bath charges. Companies take them because they think investors aren't paying attention. Just by reading the disclosures about the charges in the MD&A and the footnotes, you can judge for yourself if the charges are really "non-recurring" or "non-operational." When reviewing, ask yourself three questions:

1. Is this charge an attempt to catch up for past operating expenses not recognized originally?

2. Is this charge an attempt to recognize future expenses now, allowing the company to claim expense-free revenues later? (This happens a lot with merger-related restructuring charges.)

3. Does the company take these charges so frequently that it is impossible to understand its costs from one reporting period to the next?

Restructuring charges can cover just about anything, but most of them involve the following categories:

➤ Closing facilities.

➤ Layoffs and severance.

➤ Selling, closing, or exiting a business.

➤ Increasing reserves for litigation or other items.

➤ Writing off inventory or receivables.

➤ Writing off in-process R&D following an acquisition.

➤ Writing down long-lived assets such as goodwill.

If you understand the present and future financial statement impact of each, and the possibility for abuse, you will be way ahead of the game.

Closing facilities

This is part of a special charge taken by the company on a separate line of the income statement. In the footnotes, the company will state the size of the reserve and the amount of the reserve it used during the reporting period. If the company overstates the reserve, it reverses it in some later period. Overstating reserves is not uncommon and a dishonest company may try to just release the reserve as a reduction in the cost of revenues. The SEC made this move difficult a few years ago by requiring the disclosure of the size and use of reserves. This, in turn, makes it easier for you to see if they have reserves left over and what happened to them. Under these rules, a dishonest company will probably just try to use the reserve for operating expenses (putting regular payroll into its ledgers as severance, draining from the reserve instead of adding to the cost of revenue). You have to rely on the auditor to catch such a cheat.

Layoffs and severance

This is treated the same as closing facilities, usually in conjunction. The income statement includes the prospective cost as part of a special item. The footnotes explain what portion of the change is for employees and the yearly out-of-pocket amount used from the reserve.

Selling, closing, or exiting a business

This overlaps the facilities-closing and employee-cost items. It will be treated the same as in the financial statements, although the statements may designate a separate entry for "discontinued operations." The company may then take its sweet time actually discontinuing them, having segregated them from the operations that most investors focus on. If the company sells the asset, it will receive cash or other consideration, and it must recognize the gain or loss on sale, either as part of that charge for exiting the business or as a separate write-down. (You can bet that if a company tries to bury its profitable asset sales in operations, it won't bury its unprofitable ones there. It would rather take the heat for exiting a bad business than turning that loss into a cost of revenue.)

Increasing reserves for litigation and other risks

This may appear on the income statement as a separate item or lumped in with a larger one-time charge. The harder this information is to find, the less you should trust this company. If it doesn't state its reserves, what they cover, and their disposition, you are in big trouble. The company could have understated the risks, meaning you can get a nasty surprise when the risks come to pass. The company could also have gone the other way, overstating reserves at an opportune time, using that extra amount for other items instead of including those items in the cost of revenue. If the company isn't forthcoming, you have no way of finding out.

Writing off inventory or receivables

This write-off typically appears in the cost of revenue. (In the cash flow statement, it will appear as a separate item.) The potential for abuse occurs if the company later sells the written-off inventory or collects the written-off receivables. It is supposed to add those amounts back to the cost of revenue, but with no reserve to review in the footnotes, you won't know if this happened. This will be discussed more in Chapter 24.

Writing off in-process research and development

This was one of the big techniques to clear acquisition costs from the income statement. As will be discussed in Chapter 20, companies don't like having to put goodwill on the balance sheet, and they hate having to write it down against earnings every quarter for 20 years.

A popular dodge, particularly of companies in telecommunications, high-tech, or any field that conceivably involves research and development, was to designate a significant portion of the purchase price as "in-process research and development," declare it impaired, and write it off immediately. They have to support all this, but that has never seemed very difficult.

During the late 1990s, many companies used this charge. Cisco Systems, over a period from 1996 to 1999, acquired 30 companies for a total of $1.8 billion. It immediately wrote off $1.5 billion of the purchase price as in-process research and development. This kept it from having to account for that amount as goodwill and deduct it from earnings in the future.

With the new rules about accounting for and writing off goodwill, this method may not be used as much. Now that companies have to value and write down goodwill every year, this charade isn't as important. Although companies could have declared the assets impaired right away and taken the charge that way under the old rules, it appeared impolitic to declare immediately that you overpaid. (Admitting that most of the acquired company's value consisted of worthless in-process R&D seems like the same thing, but Cisco obviously got away with that for a long time and its shareholders never had a problem with it.)

Now, with everybody writing off goodwill, especially in the first fiscal year after the new FASB rule, the same companies may feel they can sneak in this mea culpa without consequences.

Writing down long-lived assets such as acquired goodwill

Before July 2001, the excess of the acquisition price of assets above book value was considered "goodwill," an intangible asset on the balance sheet, written down as a cost of revenues in equal amounts over 20 years. The FASB changed this, still putting goodwill on the balance sheet, but eliminating the periodic write-downs as a cost of revenues. Once a year, a company has to determine if the assets are still worth what it paid, or if they have become "impaired." The assets are written down at that time. This is explained in detail in Chapter 20.

Special warning: pre-merger charges

Beware of the pre-merger charge. Rather than doing the dirty work of putting those costs on the income statement, some companies make the target take the bullet, taking as many charges and write-downs as possible immediately before the deal closes.

It's a very smart and devious idea. The target is about to be acquired and the terms are set, so it isn't worried what its shareholders will think of the charges. This provides the acquirer with a "head start," using a bunch of assets that have been written down, reducing their recognition in the cost of revenues in future quarters.

The best defense is just to pay attention to what the acquired company does immediately before the merger. Right before Tyco International acquired CIT Group in 2001, CIT Group took a $221 million non-recurring charge.

Special warning no. 2: the little bath

The motive behind the big bath is that, once the company decides it has to report something unfavorable, it might as well report every conceivable bad thing at once, rather than spread out the bad news. In addition, if it can make things seem even worse than they are, it can benefit from later comparisons. Companies also do this through reclassifying their results. They make a change in presentation, then change the prior results to conform to the current presentation.

Usually, they do this to make the prior results look worse. The company gets to have its cake and eat it, too. For example, IBM in 1999 and 2000 trumpeted its great results. When things weren't so hot in 2001, and it was forced to come clean with regard to some slippery accounting, it reclassified some items from prior results. All of a sudden, results weren't all that great in prior years, which made 2001 look relatively better than if compared with the original results. If you look at IBM's income statements in Chapters 4 and 5, you can see how its reclassifications in 2001 ratcheted down prior results. Lucent, likewise, reclassified numbers in 1999 from its prior two fiscal years. (The tables in Chapter 11 demonstrate this.)

This is simple enough to find: The financial statements contain those magic words, "Reclassified to conform with [this year's] presentation." When you see that, get the original reports from the prior period and see what the company changed.

19 Deconstructing Restructuring: Sunbeam and Tyco International

By looking at some restructuring charges of public companies, we can understand how to interpret them and notice some of the issues that arise regarding these charges. Sunbeam went bankrupt in 1998, only months after reporting more than a year of such positive results that it was lauded as one of the turnaround stories of the decade. We discussed in Chapter 12 how revenue recognition policies created a gulf between Sunbeam's actual performance and its financial reports. It also benefited (until it got caught) from taking improper reserves and using them subsequently to cover operating expenses. Since that time, the SEC has required additional disclosures on reserves: what they are for, how much the company used, how much is left. Tyco International takes hundreds of millions of dollars in these one-time charges every year. It follows the new rules about disclosing information on reserves. Reviewing Tyco's disclosures demonstrates how carefully investors have to evaluate them to understand the charges and their future impact.

Sunbeam

At the end of 1996, shortly after Al Dunlap and a new management team took over at Sunbeam, the corporation announced a $337.6 million restructuring charge. These charges, especially when management wants to use them to distort future results, frequently occur after a merger or change in management. New management wants to tilt the odds of success in its favor and investors are even more likely than usual to ignore these charges, viewing them as criticism of the regime that got booted out.

In the press release announcing the restructuring in November 1996, Sunbeam used that old line about how the restructuring charge really doesn't cost much.

> Only 25 percent, or $75 million, of this special charge will impact cash through the payment of severance and other employee costs, lease obligations and other plant costs associated with the rationalization of excess facilities. The remaining special charges will be non-cash in nature consisting primarily of asset and inventory write-downs, losses anticipated to be incurred from divestiture of non-core businesses and increases in several reserve categories.

This is nonsense. Everything written down represented money the corporation spent that had not yet been deducted as an expense. You're not really evaluating a corporation's long-term success if you count only its expenses on profitable activities and call its failures a wash.

Most of Sunbeam's violations of accounting standards had to do with revenue recognition, a subject covered regarding Sunbeam in Chapter 12. Sunbeam also put aside $35 million of the $337.6 million reserve as a "cookie jar" to dip into to reduce operating expenses without disclosure when necessary. It's probably not a coincidence that the reserve increased from $300 million when Sunbeam announced it in November to $337.6 million when the company announced its 1996 results. It reserved $21.8 million for cooperative advertising, which it also used to offset regular operating expenses in 1997.

Sunbeam's 1996 Annual Report contained a footnote detailing the restructuring.

In conjunction with the implementation of the restructuring and growth plan, the Company recorded a pre-tax special charge to earnings of approximately $337.6 million in the fourth quarter of 1996. This amount is allocated as follows in the accompanying Consolidated Statement of Operations: $154.9 million to Restructuring, Impairment and Other Costs as further described below; $92.3 million to Cost of Goods Sold related principally to inventory write-downs from the reduction in [stock keeping units] and costs of inventory liquidation programs; $42.5 million to Selling, General and Administrative expenses principally for increases in environmental and litigation reserves and other reserve categories; and the estimated pre-tax loss on the divestiture of the Company's furniture business of approximately $47.9 million.

Amounts included in Restructuring, Impairment and Other Costs in the accompanying Consolidated Statement of Operations include cash items such as severance and other employee costs of $43.0 million, lease obligations and other exit costs associated with facility closures of $12.6 million, $7.5 million of start-up costs on back office outsourcing initiatives and other costs related to the implementation of the restructuring and growth plan. Expenditures for the cash restructuring items will be substantially completed in 1997. Non-cash Restructuring, Impairment and Other Costs include $91.8 million related to asset write-downs to net realizable value for disposals of excess facilities and equipment and non-core product lines, write-offs of redundant computer systems from the administrative back-office consolidations and outsourcing initiatives and intangibles, packaging and other asset write-downs related to exited product lines and [stock keeping unit] reductions.

There is a lot in there that investors could not possibly evaluate. Sunbeam added $92 million to the cost of goods sold and $42 million to SG&A. Therefore, when it expended this money in 1997, presumably on the items described, it would not add these amounts to the cost of revenue or SG&A. Investors, however, would be unable to check Sunbeam's honesty.

Throughout 1997, Sunbeam kept expenses artificially low by deducting operating expenses from reserves instead of adding them to the cost of revenues. You wouldn't know this from the income statement.

The cash flow statement tells a better story. When a company spends money but misclassifies it, it fools investors who focus on the earnings number. By looking at cash flow as well, the classifications make little difference (unless operating cash-flow items jump into the investing or financing sections) to the operating cash flow bottom line.

If you read Sunbeam's 1997 Annual Report, it stared you right in the face: Despite a supposedly successful restructuring and refocusing, despite $109 million in net income, Sunbeam had operating cash flow of negative $8 million. Even after cutting $70 million from net income in the subsequent restatement, cash flow improved by just $2 million. (An abridged version of Sunbeam's 1997 operating cash flow appears in Chapter 12.)

Tyco International

Tyco International has made numerous acquisitions over the past several years, and it has been criticized for its frequent use of one-time charges following mergers. (The SEC conducted a lengthy and inconclusive investigation on this subject a few years back.) The argument goes like this: A company acquiring another takes a charge for the costs of the merger (mostly lay-offs and business closings). It overstates the costs, figuring that, in the hoopla of the deal and due to the general ignorance of investors, everyone will discount the special charge. It might even get the target to take the charge itself before the merger. By booking these big costs in advance, the company can automatically appear to improve operations. With the costs of part of the business already recognized, it is easier to report a big profit later.

Tyco International's 2001 Income Statement
(amounts in millions)

	2001	2000	1999
REVENUES			
Net revenue	$34,037	$28,932	$22,496
Finance income	1,676		
Other income	335		
Earnings of Tyco Capital			
Net gain on sale of common shares of subsidiary	64	1,760	
Net gain on sale of businesses and investments	277		
TOTAL REVENUES	36,388	30,692	22,496
COSTS AND EXPENSES			
Cost of revenue	20,950	17,931	14,433
Selling, general, admin. & other costs and expenses	7,208	5,252	4,436
Interest and other financial charges, net	1,374	770	486
Provision for credit losses	116		
Merger, restructuring and other non-recurring charges, net	234	175	929
Write off of purchased in-process R&D	184		
Charges for the impairment of long-lived assets	120	99	507
TOTAL COSTS AND EXPENSES	30,186	24,227	20.791
Income taxes	(1,480)	(1,926)	(637)
Minority interest	(51)	(19)	
Extraordinary items, net of tax	(17)		(46)
Cum. effect of accounting changes, net of tax	(683)		
NET INCOME	$3,971	$4,520	$1,022

Tyco International is the reigning champion of restructuring charges, so its financial statements are a good guide to what they consist of and where they appear. Tyco's 2001 income statement includes numerous one-time items, many of which seem to be annual occurrences, as well as some one-time items tucked into operations. The latter are disclosed in the footnotes.

Obviously, the net gains, the merger and restructuring non-recurring charges, the impairment charges, and the extraordinary items are part of restructuring charges. The cost of revenue and SG&A items are also part of the charges. Even the footnote on restructuring is confusing, but it explains all the places where these charges impact the current income statement. Tyco has two separate but overlapping footnotes presenting its merger-related charges and reserves.

In Tyco's acquisitions and divestitures footnote, it disclosed that, for 2001 acquisitions, it recorded purchase accounting liabilities of $1.1 billion for the cost of integrating the acquired businesses and transaction costs. This was on acquisitions of approximately $19.5 billion. The $1.1 billion consists of $368 million for severance, $394 million for facilities, and $358 million for "other." During 2001, it utilized a little more than half this reserve, $591 million. The reserve for 2000 acquisitions was $426 million, of which Tyco used $394 million by the end of fiscal 2001. The footnote on merger and restructuring charges provided this same information, organized by segments.

It presented the following table with company-wide 2001 reserves and utilization:

Tyco International, 2001 purchase accounting liabilities (abridged) (amounts in millions)

	Severance reserve	Facilities reserve	Other reserve	Total
Original reserve	$367.9	$393.6	$358.5	$1,120.0
2001 utilization	(216.4)	(62.7)	(249.6)	(528.7)
9/30/01 balance	$151.5	$330.9	$108.9	$591.3

These reserves did not include nearly $100 million in liabilities related to the CIT acquisition; those were recorded as a liability of the successor subsidiary, Tyco Capital. Tyco disclosed this as a footnote to the table. Tyco also disclosed the size of previous years' reserves, the amounts expended from those reserves, and the amounts left. Tyco generally overestimated its reserves, and reduced the prior years' reserves in 2001 by $68.9 million. Tyco reduced goodwill and deferred tax assets by that amount on the balance sheet.

Tyco also devoted a footnote to merger, restructuring, and non-recurring charges. The footnote started with a table summarizing the net merger, restructuring, and other non-recurring charges, by business segment:

	2001	2000	1999
Electronics	$386.4	($90.9)	$643.3
Fire and security services	138.8	(11.2)	(27.2)
Healthcare and specialty products	56.7	(10.9)	419.1
Telecommunications		13.1	
Corporate	(163.4)	276.2	
TOTAL	418.5	176.3	1,035.2

This footnote, in turn, has several footnotes. The 2001 charges included $185.1 million in inventory write-offs, which were included in the cost of revenues. The 2000 charges included $11.8 million in inventory write-offs, and the 1999 charges included $106.4 million. The remainder of the 2001 charges not related to inventory, more than $233 million, was taken as the separate item on the financial statement.

Each segment for which Tyco took the charge established a series of reserves for severance, facilities, and "other." It never said what the "other" reserve covered. Each segment then reported which portion of the reserve it used during 2001. The Electronics segment has used $174.3 million of its $334.7 million in reserves. Fire and Security Services used just $31.1 million of its $107.7 million, and Healthcare and Specialty Products used only $4.4 million of its $21.7 million. It takes time to fire people and close facilities, but a lot of these reserves were probably taken late in the year. That could just be a coincidence, but in dishonest corporations such as Sunbeam and Waste Management, the companies designed late-year reserves to jump start the next year's results.

On the positive side, the SEC now requires that corporations disclose how the reserve is being used. Tyco followed that rule, but that hasn't reduced the likelihood that Tyco or any other corporation will fabricate the charges or the reporting on how the reserves are used. Most of Tyco's remaining 2000 and 2001 reserves are supposed to be used in 2002, but Tyco has been significantly overstating prior reserves; most of the positive contributions to the 2000 reserve are reversals due to earlier overestimates. For example, the $90 million credit in the Electronics segment in 2000 is primarily because it reserved too much in prior years.

Goodwill Haunting: Writing Down the Value of Merger Assets

20

The key thing to remember about merger accounting is that if you are aware of what's going on, it doesn't matter how the company accounts for the merger. Merger accounting issues trip up only investors who don't read financial statements, or who become overly dependent on reported earnings.

Prior to July 2001, companies planning to merge had to decide whether the merger was a **purchase** or a **pooling of interests**. The choice had a huge effect on future reported earnings, and the merger documents and public statements had to be worded in a certain way to be consistent with the accounting treatment planned. To get the most beneficial treatment—pooling—the merged company was also subject to limitations after the merger.

When one company acquires another—or any asset, for that matter—that asset is added to the balance sheet, along with accompanying liabilities. If a company pays an amount in excess of the net fair market value of the assets (cash, properties, receivables, etc.), the remainder of the purchase price appears on the balance sheet as goodwill.

Under pre-2001 rules, companies amortized goodwill for up to 40 years. That periodic charge reduced net income. Of course, it had no effect on cash flow and investors were free to ignore this amortization charge; but remember, nobody reads these financial statements. They all listen for the earnings number, which is now reduced by the amortization of goodwill.

To avoid the earnings charge, companies could appeal to the SEC to treat the merger as a pooling of interests. In a pooling transaction, two equal parties simply combine their assets. There is no purchase price, no premium above asset value, and no goodwill to amortize. Companies had to jump through a lot of hoops to get pooling treatment, including limits on the sale of assets for two years. This hurt operating flexibility, but it was all part of the game of keeping reported earnings pumped up.

FASB No. 141 eliminated pooling mergers as of July 2001. Now, companies account for all mergers as purchases with the excess of fair value added to the balance sheet as goodwill. In addition, the FASB also changed the rules for writing off goodwill. FASB No. 142 requires that, for all fiscal years beginning after December 15, 2001, companies must annually review the goodwill value of acquisitions and write down that value if it has become impaired. Otherwise, the goodwill is not amortized.

Companies have been invited to make big goodwill write-downs immediately. In the first annual report after the adoption of the new rules, companies can take the charge as a non-operating "change in accounting." In subsequent write-downs, it becomes an operating charge. The company must determine the amount of the write-down through some form of objective valuation analysis, such as **discounted cash flow**.

You should understand what's going on when companies take these substantial impairment charges, but it should not significantly affect your investment evaluation. On the other hand, don't ignore this as a "non-cash charge."

Your goal is always to evaluate the quality of the current results and understand how they bear on future results. If a company announces a one-time write-down of acquisition goodwill, lowering earnings by $4 per share, you should mentally add that charge back into the earnings. But the write-down represents a real attempt to determine the value of what the company bought. If the conclusion is that it significantly overpaid, that should be relevant to you. It should become part of your subjective evaluation of the quality of management. You should also take it as a signal that the results of the acquired assets will be far less than expected for the next several years. It is also important to realize, however, that by the time a company takes its big impairment charge, it has already announced some ugly financial results and had the air let out of its stock. In short, the market already knows that management blew it.

JDS Uniphase took a goodwill charge of $50 billion when it completed its year-end review of impairment during the summer of 2001, as the new rules went into effect. It had earlier announced that it was analyzing its goodwill and would take a charge of approximately $40 billion. Therefore, it took a write-down of about $40 billion by restating its third quarter (ended March 31, 2001) and another $10 billion when it announced fourth-quarter and annual results in July.

This is how its financial statements (see page 153) changed between the original and restated numbers.

JDS also restated or reclassified some other items at the same time, but the only change on the balance sheet as a result of the massive write-down was the value of intangibles.

Some of JDS's other actions resulted in other changes to its third-quarter income statement (see JDS Uniphase Income Statement on page 153), but the big difference was the charge for reduction in the value of goodwill.

JDS Uniphase Assets, 3/31/01 quarter
(dollars in millions)

	3/31/01 original	3/31/01 restated
Current assets:		
Cash and cash equivalents	$136.7	$136.7
Short-term investments	1,836.2	1,836.2
Net accounts receivable	705.4	705.4
Inventories	672.9	672.9
Deferred income taxes	71.2	71.2
Other current assets	81.3	81.3
Total current assets	3,503.7	3,503.7
Property, plant & equipment	1,193.2	1,193.2
Deferred income taxes	973.5	918.4
Intangible assets, including goodwill, net	58,443.6	18,348.6
Long term investments	918.6	204.1
Other assets	6.9	6.9
Total assets	$65,039.5	$24,174.9

JDS Uniphase Income Statement, 3/31/01 quarter
(dollars in millions)

	3/31/01 original	3/31/01 restated
Net sales	$920.1	$920.1
Cost of sales	494.2	494.2
Gross profit	425.9	425.9
Operating expenses:		
R&D	98.0	98.0
SG&A	139.1	440.8
Amortization of purchased intangibles	2,129.0	2,120.2
Reduction of goodwill		39,777.2
Acquired in-process R&D	383.7	383.7
Total operating expenses	2,749.8	42,819.9
Loss from operations	(2,323.9)	(42,394.0)

The $40 billion charge had no impact on cash flow. It was added back for cash flow purposes.

JDS Uniphase Operating Cash Flow, nine mos. ending 3/31/01 (dollars in millions)

	3/31/01 original	3/31/01 restated
Net loss	($3,205.2)	($43,759.9)
Adjustments to reconcile net loss to net cash provided by operating activities		
Reduction of goodwill		39,777.2
Acquired in-process R&D	392.6	392.6
Depreciation and amortization	4,455.3	4,446.6
Gain on sale of subsidiary	(1,770.2)	(1,770.2)
Stock compensation	21.5	21.5
Impairment of marketable sec'ies	7.5	7.5
Activity related to equity investments	138.8	853.4
Deferred income taxes	641.2	111.4
Tax benefits from stock options	90.4	90.4
Changes in operating assets & liabilities		
Accounts receivable	(248.7)	(248.7)
Inventories	(211.7)	(211.7)
Other current assets	(31.0)	(31.0)
Accounts payable, accrued liab., other accrued expenses	8.9	9.4
Net cash provided/(used) by operating activities	289.4	(11.5)

If you merely dismiss such activities as "non-cash charges," you miss some of the useful information the company is providing. JDS Uniphase did not pick that $40 billion impairment amount (or the additional subsequent amount) out of thin air. According to the MD&A in the Form 10-K, "Fair value was determined based on discounted future cash flows for the operating entities that had separately identifiable cash flows. The cash flow periods used were five years using annual growth rates of 15 percent to 60 percent, the discount rate used was 13 percent in the third quarter of 2001 and 14.5 percent in the fourth quarter of 2001, and terminal values were estimated based upon terminal growth rates of 7 percent."

Assuming growth rates of 15 to 60 percent, these assets would bring in at least $40 billion less than the goodwill attributed to them. With those liberal growth rates, JDS said that changes in assumptions "may change in the near term resulting in the need to further write down goodwill." In fact, that's exactly what happened: JDS had to write down the remaining goodwill even more. JDS was sending you a message: We're looking at a long period in which these assets will not perform anywhere near their cost.

Of course, most of this was not a surprise to the stock market. In mid-2000, JDS Uniphase stock traded for more than $130 per share. The day before it made its initial disclosure that it would write off a big dollar amount of goodwill in April 2001, it traded for $24 per share. It dropped briefly after this announcement, but returned to $24 per share. As more news came out, however, and it sunk in that JDS's write-down was an admission of inferior operating results for the present and future, in addition to a technical piece of bookkeeping business, the stock continued to plunge, dropping into the $5–6 per share range in early 2002.

These write-downs do not affect real earnings or cash flow, but they are an admission of some bad business dealing. They also constitute management's best guess that business is going to stink for a long time.

21

Pro Forma Results: Friend *and* Foe

Pro forma results were very popular during the late 1990s, which means they have to be very unpopular now. Pro forma results are simply financial results reported in some form other than that required by the SEC and generally accepted accounting principles. Pro forma results can help you make comparisons that might otherwise be more difficult. They can also mislead you; many pro forma presentations are nothing more than slick public relations jobs by the company.

The current backlash against abusive accounting will ultimately do more harm than good to pro forma results. You should be in favor of anything companies do to provide more information. You should be against anything they do to confuse or mislead you, but your defense should be your skepticism, intelligence, and understanding of their tactics. Discouraging companies from reformulating their results won't keep them from trying to spin those results. If you can, take their charity, disregard what you should disregard, and take advantage of helpful information.

The controversy over pro forma reporting exists solely because investors don't read financial statements. If you get your information from a news report or the headline of a press release, you can easily be misled. If you read the results, the company can add any summary or reformulation it wants.

You should be developing your own pro forma measures. We have discussed, for example, how measures such as employee exercise of options, increased accounts payable, and deferred taxes improve operating cash flow. (This will be discussed further in Chapter 30.) You should discount or eliminate those things, because they don't count for much, or are even negatives, for the future.

This issue comes up because companies are required, in their Form 10-Qs and 10-Ks to present their results in conformance with GAAP. They file the quarterly reports 45 days after the quarter and the annual report 90 days after the fiscal year. The company usually issues a press release announcing the quarterly results a few weeks after the quarter ends. These releases often don't include cash flow but do provide, in addition to an income statement, a lot of text in which the company tries to spin the results to look as good as possible, which can include taking out some things and recategorizing others.

If you don't go further than the headlines, this is all you can learn from AOL Time Warner's fourth-quarter results from 2001:

➤ AOL Time Warner reports results for full year and fourth quarter.

➤ Performance in line with preliminary results announced on January 7.

➤ Full year normalized EBITDA up 18 percent to $9.9 billion; total revenues increase 6 percent to $38.2 billion.

➤ Fourth quarter normalized EBITDA grows 14 percent to $2.8 billion; quarterly revenues up 4 percent to $10.6 billion; subscription revenues climb 16 percent to $4.4 billion.

Normalized? **EBITDA**? What happened to net income or earnings per share?

The first paragraph of the press release tells you some of this, but also lets you know that AOL Time Warner is going to use its own judgment about what it will include and exclude in the press release. "Unless otherwise specified, results discussed herein have been adjusted to normalize out the effect of merger-related costs and significant and non-recurring items that have occurred in each period, which are discussed in more detail in the accompanying footnotes." Here are some additional chilling words if you think they'll tell you if they omit something that could possibly be important: "It should be noted that unusual or non-recurring items might occur in any period and users of this financial information should consider the types of events and transactions for which adjustments have been made."

AOL Time Warner also tells you in the press release that, in this case, "pro forma" means the 2000 results were prepared assuming the AOL Time Warner merger was in effect January 1, 2000. If you read the annual report, it tells you the same thing, including pro forma combined AOL/Time Warner results for 2000, as well as GAAP results for AOL only for 2000. The footnotes to the financial statements in the press release, which most companies do not include in press releases, further explain how it reclassified certain items.

That is a helpful use of pro forma results. Certainly, there may be reasons why AOL and Time Warner, as separate companies, would have performed differently than after the merger. Nevertheless, if you are looking at 2001 results, which are combined because the companies merged on January 11, 2001, and you want to compare them to the year-before period, would you rather have imperfect pro forma 2000 combined results, or be staring at AOL-only financial statements? Make sure you read all disclosures that come with pro forma results. The companies know they can't substitute these for GAAP results, so they are very careful not to give the impression they are trying to trick anybody. They explain very clearly the differences between the pro forma results and the GAAP results, and then hope you will ignore those differences. Find out for yourself what's included, what's excluded, and what's recategorized. Then decide if the numbers are good enough for you to use in an investment evaluation.

Because there are no rules about pro forma results, companies can include and exclude whatever they want. One recent helpful example involved September 11-related expenses. The FASB, which usually takes eons to make any kind of decision, determined shortly after the terrorist attacks that expenses as a result of the attacks should be considered as part of operations and not one-time charges. In the pro forma results, some companies included a separate item with the September 11-related expenses and gave investors an idea of the magnitude of those expenses and what the results looked like without them.

On the other hand, we discussed merger and restructuring charges in Chapters 15 and 18–20. If some company wants to take those out of its pro forma results, you should look at the GAAP results, or put those charges back in.

Earnings Before Interest, Taxes, Depreciation, and Amortization (EBITDA)

Earnings Before Interest, Taxes, Depreciation, and Amortization (EBITDA) first became popular in 1988, as the first post-leveraged buyout companies went public. Most takeovers in that era were cash deals, mostly with borrowed money. When these companies tapped the public equity markets a few years later, their interest expense ate up most of their earnings. To encourage investors to invest in these highly leveraged companies, they wanted investors to ignore the debt and focus on the strength of operations. Time Warner was one of the first large companies to advocate ignoring earnings for EBITDA. In its acquisition of Warner Communications, Time had to take on huge debt. Much like the AOL deal, the "acquirer" for accounting and PR purposes ended up being the target. Along with the amortization of goodwill, the merged company was not able to report positive earnings for a long time.

EBITDA is a popular measure now because many big companies face large reductions in earnings for the long-term future as a result of acquisition-created goodwill. Because WorldCom emphasized EBITDA over other measures of financial performance, there may be a general backlash against EBITDA.

Companies using EBITDA contend that it is similar to cash flow. You're better off looking at cash flow. EBITDA doesn't track changes in working capital, so a company padding results with uncollectible receivables is still free to wreak havoc with EBITDA. You should also look at a whole financial statement instead of just one number. These entries are not all created equal. Just as EBITDA tells you to disregard depreciation and amortization, other elements of the cash flow statements need to be considered.

Yahoo! is a company that has always emphasized its pro forma results. For the first quarter of 2002, Yahoo! emphasized that its EBITDA was $24.4 million, a big increase from the year-ago quarter total of only $858,000. Net income didn't even make it into the first paragraph of the press release. Net income, it said, was $10.5 million ($0.02 per share). But even that number excluded a $64.1 million charge for impairment of long-lived assets, in conjunction with newly adopted SFAS No. 142. With the impairment charge included, Yahoo! had a loss of $53 million ($0.09 per share).

To see the differences between EBITDA and cash flow (and between standardized GAAP-style results and pro forma results), you don't have to look beyond Yahoo!'s first-quarter results. According to Yahoo!, here is how it calculates EBITDA:

From the Notes to Yahoo!'s Consolidated Statement of Operations (amounts in thousands)

	3/31/2002	3/31/2001
Reported loss from operations	$(4,175)	$(32,768)
Depreciation and amortization	22,955	30,211
Stock compensation expense	5,621	3,415
EBITDA	24,401	858

If you look at operating cash flow, however, you see how Yahoo!'s position actually deteriorated since the year-ago period.

From the Notes to Yahoo!'s Summary Cash Flow Data (amounts in thousands)

	3/31/2002	3/31/2001
Net loss	$(53,645)	$(11,486)
Adjustments to reconcile net loss to net cash provided by operating activities		
Depreciation and amortization	22,955	30,211
Tax benefits from stock options	6,804	2,058
Cumulative effect of accounting change	64,120	
Earnings in equity interests	(4,300)	(614)
Minority interests	(212)	(229)
Other non-cash items	7,483	19,052
Change in working capital	4,238	32,061
Net cash provided by operating activities	47,443	71,053

Even when taking out the deductions for amortization and depreciation, Yahoo!'s operating activities provided more cash in the first quarter of 2001 than it did in the first quarter of 2002.

In general, you should take all the information a company gives you, but don't substitute the shorthand of its press release or of a news report for your ability to read for yourself and understand the company's operations.

22

Accounting for Stock Options

During the bull market of the 1990s, the use of stock options as compensation dramatically increased, especially for technology companies. The usual situation was that employees would receive part of their pay in the form of options to buy the company's stock. The exercise price was the market price on the day the options were issued, or a price based on some formula taking into account the recent historical price of the stock. (For tech companies with surging stock prices, any historical formula increased the amount of money employees immediately made, at least on paper.)

Even though stock options are an increasingly important part of employee compensation, they are not treated as a compensation expense like salaries, pension contributions, or medical benefits. The options do not appear as an expense on the income statement when they are issued or when they are exercised.

This has become very controversial. The options, even before exercised, have a value that can be calculated. The FASB considered rules for accounting for options on the income statement in the mid-1990s, but withdrew in the face of heavy lobbying by business. With the current emphasis by Congress and investors on the transparency of financial statements, there is discussion again about changing the accounting.

The big problem with options is a matter of perception. For some reason, investors think that issuing stock doesn't cost as much as paying out money. If you asked 100 investors whether they'd rather have a company pay its employees another $1 million or give them options worth that amount, all 100 would probably choose giving them the options. This is because investors forget that, when they buy stock, they own a portion of the company. Because the stake that individual investors own in companies is so small, they marginalize the cost of making it smaller.

The same investors would feel differently if the impact could be made more personal. Say you paid $50,000 to buy a one-third interest in a restaurant; the company gives you 100 of 300 outstanding shares. It's a very profitable restaurant and because of distributions you receive or information you get that similar restaurant values are soaring, the value of that one-third is now approximately $100,000. Employees need more compensation. Do you want to give them the cash or issue them 100 new shares, raising the total outstanding to 400? If you have a share of a growing enterprise, you generally want to keep the ownership to yourself. Anyone who ever owned a successful business would find the cash cheaper to give than a portion of the ownership.

As with most controversial accounting issues, the information is already disclosed. You just have to know where to find it.

Where to find options information

You can improve your understanding of a company's operations by using the diluted shares rather than basic shares for per-share calculations. Microsoft, for example, reported earnings per share of $1.38 for its 2001 fiscal year, ended June 30, 2001. This is based on net income of $7.3 billion and 5.35 billion outstanding shares. Microsoft had 233 million additional shares in the form of exercisable employee options, so the company's diluted earnings per share was $1.32.

Even this number may underestimate the effect of stock-option exercise. In lieu of including the cost of options on the income statement, companies can choose, under current rules, to prepare a pro forma set of results treating the options as expenses, and bury it in the footnotes. That's what everybody chooses to do. For example, Microsoft disclosed in its 2001 Annual Report footnote on employee stock options that its employees held 331 million vested options and the company had 550 million shares available for future grants. These options have a present value, even if they are currently out of the money. This value is determined by a formula by economics professors named Black and Scholes. The formula takes into account the exercise period, exercise and market price, and stock-price volatility. Under SFAS No. 123, Microsoft, as did nearly all companies, valued its options based on the **Black-Scholes model** and recognized the cost ratably over the vesting period. Along with the value of previous years' options, Microsoft's basic earnings would have been $0.95 and diluted earnings would have been $0.91.

With that large of an effect, you can see why companies protest so vociferously to measures that require more prominent reporting of the effect of valuing stock options like other compensation.

Repricing options

The argument for stock-option compensation is that tying employee compensation to stock performance motivates them. So if it doesn't work and the company's stock price falls, the employees are out of luck, right?

Wrong. Companies routinely reprice the options when their stock price drops. The FASB requires that companies expense the repriced options on the income statement. This rule has a giant loophole, though, one so big that you will rarely see such an expense. If the company merely cancels the options and issues new ones that are identical except for a lower exercise price—the same effect as repricing the original options—it doesn't have to treat the value of the options as an expense.

Tax benefits from stock options

One of the reasons legislators get so incensed about the lack of income-statement treatment of options is that, in contrast to the financial statements in which options would hurt results if included as a cost, companies can take full tax advantage of their cost. When the option is exercised, the company counts, as a deductible expense, the difference between the cost of the options at their exercise price (using the Black-Scholes model during the exercise year) and their market price. For companies that use options liberally to compensate employees and have rising stock prices, the tax benefit is huge. For Microsoft, this was more than $2 billion during fiscal 2001. (You can find this out by looking at the operating cash flow. When Microsoft stock was in its halcyon days, the tax break was eye-popping. In fiscal 2000, it was $5.5 billion.) When you hear that old complaint about a huge high-flying company not paying any federal taxes, and you couldn't hear anyone in Congress in early 2002 mention Enron without bringing that up, this tends to be the reason.

The tax benefit also has a favorable impact on operating cash flow, although you should consider discounting it. The benefit is for real but its basis is really the company's buoyant stock price, not the strength of its operations. You would hope that the strength of its operations *caused* the stock price to rise, but as soon as the stock runs out of gas, options activity slows or stops, and the values used for calculating the size of the benefit become smaller.

Issuing shares versus buying shares for the exercise of options

Where do the shares come from that companies give out to employees when they exercise their options? It can buy them or issue them. Companies that purchase the shares in the open market prevent current shareholders from getting diluted. IBM repurchases stock on the open market and holds it for stock option use, in the meantime, lowering the number of shares outstanding. Young companies whose stocks were on wild, speculative rides, such as Cisco or Sun Microsystems, during those heady days of the late 1990s, didn't have the money to buy that stock, and probably not the conviction to pay the prices those shares were commanding in the open market. When that is the case, recognize that these options will dilute your ownership.

The amount of attention given to employee stock options is excessive. Yes, there is a good argument that the tax benefit is excessive. (As an investor in a company receiving that benefit, though, *you* benefit.) And yes, there is a good argument that the cost of options should appear in the income statement. But you can find the information, if you are one of those rare individual investors who read the financial statements and know where to look.

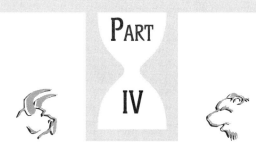

The Balance Sheet... and Beyond

After years of getting too little attention, the balance sheet is attracting a lot of scrutiny, thanks to Enron. Investors ignored the balance sheet for too long, to their peril. The balance sheet is where risks and contingencies are revealed. On the positive side, the increased scrutiny on corporate financial reporting has pushed companies to reveal more information in the balance sheets.

The final chapter of this Part provides more information about the cash flow statement. The cash flow statement is your secret weapon in evaluating companies, both as a separate measure and as a means of checking the results reported in the income statement. Except for misclassification on some kinds of cash flow, discussed in that chapter, it is very difficult for companies to manipulate cash flow.

Accounts Receivable and the Oxford Incident

23

As we have discussed throughout the book, accounts receivable is a neglected number on the balance sheet that is uncannily accurate in revealing business difficulties and even otherwise-concealed fraud. In Chapters 11 and 12, we examined in detail how soaring accounts receivable balances at Lucent and Sunbeam foretold serious problems well before investors took their lumps.

There are four ways to use the accounts receivable number to evaluate corporate results:

1. Growth of receivables relative to growth in revenues.

2. Number of days of outstanding receivables over successive periods.

3. The growth in the reserve for uncollectible receivables compared to the growth in total receivables.

4. Operating cash flow compared with net income (because the growth in receivables is deducted from operating cash flow).

Let's see how to make these evaluations on Oxford Health Plans, an HMO company that became phenomenally successful in the mid-1990s until its receivables problems brought it down. New management restored a fundamentally sound business, but the company's stock has never returned to the levels at which it traded during the summer of 1997.

The Oxford story

Oxford Health Plans is in the managed-care business. It collects premiums, usually from employers who provide access to healthcare as an employment benefit, and pays a portion of those premiums to facilities it has established, as well as to third-party health-care providers.

By 1995, Oxford was considered a huge success by Wall Street. It was growing by 50 percent a year and its stock price (adjusting for splits) had tripled in 1995, ending the year at $30 per share.

The winning streak appeared to continue during 1996 and 1997. By mid-July 1997, Oxford stock reached $89 per share. Revenues and earnings soared during this period:

From Oxford Health Plans Income Statements (abridged) (amounts in millions, except per-share amounts)

	1996 Q1	1996 Q2	1996 Q3	1996 Q4	1997 Q1	1997 Q2
Revenues	$658.1	$725.3	$811.3	$880.3	$987.3	$1,061.9
Net income	18.5	22.5	26.6	32.0	34.4	37.2
EPS	.25	.28	.33	.39	.42	.45

There were rumblings of some problems, but nothing anyone took seriously. The New York Attorney General complained about Oxford's tardy reimbursement, and the company disclosed that it had some problems implementing a complex new computer system to handle its surging growth. If anybody even thought about these problems, they probably figured, in such a heady atmosphere, "What great problems to have; they're growing too fast for their back office to keep up!"

On October 27, 1997, Oxford dropped a bomb on investors. It would have to increase its reserves for medical claims by $50 million. More important, it would have to lower revenues compared to estimates by $111 million for the quarter, for "adjustments to membership resulting from delayed premium bills." Oxford's stock dropped from $68 per share to $25 per share on the release of this news, and it never really recovered. By the following summer, amid the continuing reports about how bad things really were inside Oxford Health, the stock dropped as low as $6 per share. A management purge and long-executed turnaround restored some credibility to the company, but that took years.

The glitch to end all glitches

Subsequently, shareholders learned that, behind the façade, the operations of Oxford were a comedy of errors. No one could operate the computers. Bills never got sent out. Repayment to health-care providers lagged. Oxford eventually had to pay providers before it even collected premiums from members. Finally, huge numbers of free-riding members quit the program without ever being billed.

During those six great quarters before the fall, how much could you have figured out on your own?

From Oxford Health Plans Financial Statements (abridged) (amounts in millions, except for percentages and days)

	1996 Q1	1996 Q2	1996 Q3	1996 Q4	1997 Q1	1997 Q2
Net premiums receivable	$134.7	$123.2	$139.9	$315.1	$388.2	$421.8
Allowance for doubtful accounts	3.52	2.04	2.46	???	???	???
Revenue growth	22%	10%	12%	9%	12%	8%
Receivables growth	40%	(9%)	14%	125%	23%	9%
Days receivables outstanding	18	15	15	32	35	35
Operating cash flow	$21.9	$119.9	$140.7	$4.7	($23.0)	($84.2)

We have to make the calculations for growth of revenues, receivables, and the allowance ourselves, along with the days receivables outstanding. Each of the growth numbers is compared quarter-to-quarter, although you could make the same calculation year-over-year. In fact, when dealing with a seasonal business, that would be advisable. But Oxford was reporting such fast growth that any relative comparison will do.

The most obvious tip-off is the giant increase in accounts receivable during the fourth quarter of 1996, from $140 million the quarter before to $315 million at the end of the year. (Incidentally, Oxford stopped disclosing its reserve for doubtful accounts that quarter.) The company explained the reason for the giant increase, attributing it "primarily as the result of delays in billings caused by conversion of certain of the Company's operations to a new computer system."

The 1996 Annual Report provided numerous descriptions about the temporary disruptions caused by converting to the new system. With the company's success and record for growth, and without the benefit of hindsight, it wouldn't have been unreasonable to give Oxford the benefit of the doubt for a little while.

But when do you stop letting the company make excuses? The receivables rose still more in the first quarter of 1997, to $388 million. The company again blamed billing delays caused by conversion to the new computer system. The same thing happened in the second quarter, when receivables rose to almost $422 million. The company said the increase was "primarily as the result of delays earlier this year in billing caused by conversion of certain of the Company's operations to a new computer system, but receivables have decreased slightly, measured by days in operating revenues outstanding, as the Company's billing has returned to normal cycles."

By the end of the second quarter, it was clearly time for Oxford to give that excuse a rest. Receivables growth was still outpacing revenue growth, and days of revenue outstanding had not declined but had stabilized at 35 days, more than twice the amount of the year-earlier period.

Furthermore, operating cash flow pointed to a fundamentally sick operation. Although operating cash flow increased during the first three quarters of 1996, a large component of that cash flow was an increase in medical costs payable. As I have said several times, improving cash flow by not paying your bills will not help for long. During the fourth quarter of 1996, operating cash flow fell to an anemic $4.7 million. Operating cash flow was negative for the first two quarters of 1997.

If you look at the operating cash flow, along with the contributions made by changes in accounts receivable and medical costs payable, you can see how the situation was even worse than the gross operating cash-flow numbers indicated:

From Oxford Health Plans Financial Statements (abridged)
(amounts in millions, except for percentages and days)

	1996 Q1	1996 Q2	1996 Q3	1996 Q4	1997 Q1	1997 Q2
Operating cash flow	$21.9	$119.9	$140.7	$4.7	$(23.0)	$(84.2)
Change in accounts receivable	(39.1)	11.2	(17.4)	(173.5)	(73.1)	(33.6)
Change in medical costs payable	65.4	61.5	98.4	98.5	33.4	(125.1)

Without the contribution from owing more money to healthcare providers, Oxford's cash flow would been much worse.

Growing companies will encourage you to believe that a growing operation will have a growing receivable balance. True enough, but inefficient and corrupt companies have growing receivable balances as well. If the balance itself isn't a red flag, the other receivable-related numbers will help you figure it out.

Even in a fast-growing company, if receivables are growing faster than revenues, or the reserve is not growing as fast as the receivable balance, or the company suddenly stops keeping a reserve or telling you about it, or the number of days receivable outstanding increases, then the company has a problem. If history is any judge, you can learn about this problem before anyone else, using just this publicly available information.

Inventory

24

Inventory will generally play a smaller role than accounts receivable in your analysis of a company's operations. There are, however, three situations in which we need to be aware of what's going on with inventory. First, a company can improve its net income if it can find a way to boost inventory at the end of the period. Second, inventory write-downs, like many other forms of accounting mischief in connection with mergers, can be used to set up artificial improvements in future earnings. Third, rising inventory can tip you off to a coming write-down or, worse, a fundamental operating problem.

The boost

There is a relationship between inventory and net income that is not well understood. Net income, of course, is revenues minus costs. Costs can come from many sources, but the cost of products comes from the inventory number. The company takes the inventory balance at the beginning of the period, adds the amount spent on inventory during the period, then subtracts the ending inventory amount. Therefore, if a company can make the final inventory number larger, that changes the equation, leading to a lower cost of revenue.

In the rare instances in which companies directly try to add to that ending number, they use startlingly crooked methods.

My favorite was the trick employed by MiniScribe, the long-gone maker of disk drives. That company, to make the quarterly numbers, would pack garbage and even bricks into boxes and mix them in with the real inventory. It actually managed to get Coopers & Lybrand to provide some clean audit letters while it valued inventory in this fashion.

This would be a difficult problem for investors to uncover in advance, but you can use tools similar to those you use with accounts receivable to help. Is the **gross margin** improving coincident to an increase in inventory? Is inventory rising faster than revenues? Has the number of days inventory outstanding increased? (You will need to make some of your own calculations here, either figuring out gross margin on your own, or figuring the number of days inventory outstanding.)

If a company has some inventory it will never sell, failure to write off that inventory will have the same effect.

Failure to write off inventory

When a company discovers that it will be unable to sell some portion of its inventory, it has to immediately recognize the cost of that inventory on the income statement and write it down on the balance sheet. If a company delays the write-off, it can keep its net income higher during that period.

In April 2001, Cisco Systems announced a giant inventory write-off. In addition to a variety of other restructuring charges, it wrote off $2.25 billion in the value of its inventory, adding that amount to the cost of sales on the income statement. Cisco had previously tried to give investors the impression that it was a safe haven among Internet infrastructure companies. Investors had figured otherwise by this time, and the company finally threw in the towel. In March 2000, Cisco traded at $80 per share. By March 2001, it dropped below $20. With the market for technology and Internet companies (and Cisco was both) in tatters, it traded for $42 per share as late as January 24, 2001. Is there a possibility it delayed its write-down, keeping results artificially inflated?

After very gradual increases in inventory over the previous two years, Cisco's inventory began accumulating rapidly during 2000.

Cisco's Inventory
(amounts in millions)

Quarter ended	Inventory
1/27/01	$2,533
10/28/00	1,956
7/31/00	1,232
4/29/00	878
1/29/00	695
10/30/99	655
7/31/99	652
5/1/99	621
1/23/99	472
10/24/98	375
7/25/98	362
4/25/98	308
1/24/98	267

For the quarter ended April 28, 2001, Cisco's inventory was more than $1.9 billion, and that's *after* taking the $2.25 billion write-down. It seems a year after everyone recognized that the Internet boom had stalled, the folks at Cisco were ordering every piece of equipment and raw material possible for orders that no longer existed.

Until early 2001, Cisco's revenues grew by at least 10 percent per quarter. For the most part, until 2000, its inventories grew more slowly. For the July 2000 quarter, which was also the end of Cisco's 2000 fiscal year, inventory grew by more than $350 million. Neither sales nor cost of sales grew nearly as fast as inventory.

In December 2000, when the company announced its first quarter 2001 results, it was clear that Cisco was no longer that lean, disciplined company incapable of making mistakes and impervious to economic or industry conditions. Revenues rose $700 million from the previous quarter, to $6.5 billion. The cost-of-sales numbers, however, were disturbing. The cost of sales rose only slightly, by less than $300 million, to $2.37 billion. Inventory, however, jumped to more than $1.9 billion. (By the time Cisco announced its January quarterly results in March 2001, the market already knew the company was in trouble. The April write-down merely confirmed it.)

Oddly, the general reaction to the April write-down was almost naively optimistic. Most commentators assumed that, for a write-down that large, Cisco must have decided to take the big bath and make things seem worse than they were, so it could sell some of that written-off inventory and book extra profits in future quarters.

I think this gave Cisco's management too much credit. The inventory situation had clearly gotten out of control. Any deviousness by the company was probably in delaying the charge, squeezing an extra quarter or two of favorable results out of an artificially smaller cost-of-revenues because of bloated end-of-quarter inventory numbers.

Incidentally, as with other one-time charges, don't fall into the trap of considering this a non-operating expense. If you owned a restaurant and habitually over-ordered food shipments and had to throw a bunch of rotting food away, that's part of your operations. Whether it is bad management or conservative planning, you can't assume that it won't happen again, especially if there's a chance you as an investor won't learn about such problems until they have gotten out of hand.

Using a write-down to improve future results

This is what everyone thought Cisco was doing with its $2.25 billion write-down in April 2001. It swore that wasn't the case, and its results in the year since have been bad enough that it seems unlikely the company did anything to dress them up. On the other hand, if Cisco did this, it would be far from the first time a company ever tried it.

Tyco International, as we discussed in Chapter 19, has done a great deal of acquisitions over the past several years and takes hundreds of millions of dollars a year in restructuring charges. A significant component of these charges is writing down the inventory of the company it is acquiring. In 1999 to 2001, Tyco wrote off $300 million in inventory it acquired. This all went immediately to the bottom line, because it was applied to reducing the cost of revenue.

As long as you can keep acquiring companies, this creates the opportunity for some very creative bookkeeping. Say your $1-billion-in-sales company is breaking even. You buy another $1-billion-in-sales company that's breaking even. It has $300 million in inventory, which you write down to $100 million. Your next results will show a $200 million profit for the combined enterprise. If you sell off that written-down inventory, all that money is profit, too, because it no longer appears on the balance sheet.

How could a company get away with this? The balancing transaction is a $200 million restructuring charge to reduce the value of the inventory. If you ignore that or consider it outside operations, you can fall into this trap. You must either consider restructuring charges as operating costs, or steer clear of a company that is so active in acquisitions that you really can't figure out where the profits come from.

25 The Four Horsemen of the Off-Balance-Sheet Apocalypse

No factor contributed as much to Enron's demise, or conjured up more images of secret corporate maneuvers, than off-balance-sheet transactions. If you know where to look and read carefully, you can factor off-balance-sheet liabilities into your evaluation. In addition, the combination of potential FASB action, which will be both slow and modest, and pressure on companies to disclose more in the wake of Enron's collapse will make such transactions easier to spot in the future.

Four kinds of transactions have the potential to create risks and liabilities off the balance sheet:

1. special purpose entities (SPEs).

2. synthetic leases.

3. pension liabilities.

4. other commitments and contingencies.

All off-balance-sheet transactions have legitimate purposes, but they also carry the potential of allowing the company to keep debt off the balance sheet or expenses off the income statement.

Special purpose entities

This is one of the ugly loopholes in the accounting rules. Normally, if a company owns more than 50 percent of any entity, its results are included in the financial statements. In fact, companies usually have to count 100 percent of the assets, liabilities, gains, and losses, and then make provisions to subtract the minority interest. Even minority interests are included in the financial statements, marked at market or cost.

Special purpose entities are supposed to trade a transfer of assets for freedom of the company from liability for the debt incurred. The abuse occurs when the company is still on the hook for the debt. After Enron went bankrupt because of its SPE exposure, companies are providing greater disclosure. This is described in Chapter 26.

Synthetic leases

As you know from your own finances, if you rent, you don't own anything. If you own a house, it is an asset, but your mortgage is a liability. The situation is the same for companies. A synthetic lease—companies rarely call it by this name until after their attempts to hide it have failed—allows a company to treat a property purchase as a lease on the financial statements, but gain the tax advantages of ownership. A third party officially owns the property, but the third party is usually a financial institution. The purchase of the property is accomplished primarily through debt, which the company must someday pay off. To keep the deal off the balance sheet, the term of the loan/lease has to be less than seven years.

This is why synthetic leases are a ticking time bomb. Just as if you take a short-term mortgage, you can run into trouble if you can't refinance or roll it over. If interest rates rise or property values fall, you can be in real financial distress. The same is true when companies enter into these arrangements, but you would never know it from looking at the balance sheet.

We will look at an example of a company abusing synthetic leases in Chapter 27. Dollar General had everyone convinced it could grow fast, open a lot of discount stores, and keep capital spending small. No one noticed the $500 million in synthetic leases disclosed but not included on the balance sheet.

Pension liabilities

Corporate pension plans consist of contractual obligations for a company to make certain future payments to retirees. If the pension plan is funded with too much money (more than current estimates of future payouts, including future returns on current assets), the company doesn't have to contribute any more. If the plan is underfunded, the company has to put in money at some time in the future.

In the 1980s and 1990s, the generally good financial markets (particularly in contrast with the previous periods) led to big accumulations in pension plans. Companies didn't have to make contributions and, in fact, could claim the surplus amounts in the pension plans as net income, even though they couldn't access that money. As investment returns improved, companies generally altered the assumptions under the plans, further reducing the likelihood they would have to make contributions to their plans and increasing the likelihood of a contribution to net income.

Now, in an unfavorable investing climate, investors have to assess the opposite problem. If a plan becomes underfunded, that constitutes a real liability of the company, and it may not appear on the balance sheet. In Chapter 28, we will review the pension-related disclosures in the most recent annual reports of GE, Verizon, and Qwest.

Other commitments and contingencies

In addition to debt taken on for specific purposes, companies like the flexibility of having lines of credit available. They negotiate with banks and other financial institutions, paying up-front fees (and usually holding out the carrot of other business) to contractually obligate lenders to keep certain amounts of credit available for extended periods.

You know the adage that banks like to lend only to people who don't need money? This creates big risks for banks. When the company is rolling in dough and the deal mill is hopping, everyone wants to extend credit, so the company gets the banks on the hook with lines of credit. Then, when the business falls apart, the company is teetering on the brink of bankruptcy, and no one in their right mind would throw any more money down the drain, the bank is obligated to provide the loan. Enron, in its death throes, chewed up about $3 billion from J.P. Morgan Chase and some other banks, much of which those banks will probably never recover.

In evaluating an investment in a bank stock, look at the MD&A on the subject of corporate credit risk. Citigroup, in its 2001 Annual Report, has a section titled "Corporate Credit Risk." It includes a table breaking out its credit portfolio into "direct outstandings" and "unfunded commitments." Unfunded commitments ($194 billion) nearly equaled direct outstandings ($215 billion). (In 2000, Citigroup did not include this table in its MD&A.) In the footnotes, under "pledged assets, collateral and commitments," Citigroup included another $24 billion in financial guarantees it provided, most of which were not covered by collateral.

Other kinds of binding future commitments also appear in the financial reports, but not on the balance sheet. For example, AOL Time Warner, in addition to $1 billion per year in operating leases, has outstanding contracts of $28.3 billion, $12.2 billion of that due in 2002. The contracts, explained in the "commitments and contingencies" footnote and also in the MD&A under "contractual and other obligations," involve the company obtaining programming, purchasing AOL Europe, paying narrowband and broadband network providers, and operating leases.

No consideration of off-balance-sheet liabilities would be complete without examining Enron. We discussed in the Introduction how a review of Enron's operating cash flow revealed some big problems and a number of questions that couldn't be answered. Although Enron's bankruptcy has caused other companies to rush to provide better disclosure of their off-balance-sheet liabilities and other controversial items, we should finish a discussion of off-balance-sheet liabilities with a review of Enron's final financial statements. This appears in Chapter 29.

Special Purpose Entities

26

Special purpose entities (SPEs) are an exception to the general rule of consolidating corporate results. Normally, if a company owns more than 50 percent of an enterprise, its assets and liabilities appear on the balance sheet.

SPEs developed for a legitimate purpose. Say a company wanted to engage in a high-risk venture without putting the whole company in jeopardy. If it set up a separate entity, and everyone knew the company would not be responsible beyond its investment for the entity's debts, the arrangement was fine. Likewise, if a debt-laden company with unencumbered assets wanted to get a loan, it could obtain better terms freed from the rest of its capital structure.

This led to a series of rules that exalted form over substance. Someone other than the company has to be an investor, but the company can own up to 97 percent, as long as it doesn't have voting control. SPEs, especially those that mean trouble for investors, usually have the following features:

➤ The company sets up the SPE, owning up to 97 percent.

➤ It sells an asset to the SPE.

➤ The 3-percent owner is usually some interested party, such as a financial institution or some employees that can be counted out to nominally have voting control but not interfere with the company.

➤ The SPE borrows heavily, paying the company for the asset out of the loan proceeds.

➤ To get the loans for the SPE, the company may offer some sweetener, such as guaranteeing the loans or otherwise backing them up with some assets or securities of the company.

This last step is where the abuse occurs. If the SPE is not really completely separate from the company, and its debts are guaranteed or somehow connected to the company, it is no longer sheltering the company from liability. It is sheltering the company only from the *appearance* of liability. The investors are the potential victims, especially because the complex terms of SPE loans usually leave the company on the hook only at the worst possible time, for example, if the company's stock price falls, or the value of the SPE's asset falls, or the company's credit rating falls. Enron collapsed almost immediately after its falling stock price and credit rating triggered its liability for some SPE loans.

Certain businesses are especially active users of SPEs. One benefit of Enron's bankruptcy is that companies reporting annual results in the months following provided more and clearer disclosures of SPE exposure. In general, however, if you know where to look, the fact that SPEs do not appear on the balance sheet will not prevent you from finding out about them.

Banks and SPEs

Banks and other financial institutions use SPEs to package and sell loans, mostly consumer loans such as credit cards and mortgages. Some banks are also dumping their troubled loans in

SPEs, part of the general effort to use SPEs and the securities-held-for-sale designation to hide weaknesses in the loan portfolio. Correctly, banks point out that they could not extend so much consumer credit—as if we should assume that is automatically a good thing—if they couldn't raise capital by packaging and selling loans. But if the bank retains any kind of liability if these transferred loans go bad, all this does is drastically increase the bank's exposure while lowering the profile of its activities.

PNC Financial, the Pittsburgh-based bank, restated 2001 results shortly after releasing them in January 2002. The Federal Reserve Board objected to PNC's off-balance-sheet treatment of three subsidiaries created to hold and sell distressed loans. PNC had to reduce 2001 net income by $155 million.

The Enron fallout will probably lead to better voluntary disclosure of SPEs, if not rules eventually requiring better disclosure or limiting their use. PNC's disclosure of this liability before the Fed stepped in is disturbing, both for the risks it suggested and for the vague and confusing way it disclosed them.

Banks frequently use the held-for-sale category to stash bad loans. PNC took this to a new level. Its 2000 balance sheet showed $1.6 billion in loans for sale. The MD&A on "loans held for sale" said the reduction (from $3.5 billion in 1999)

> was primarily due to its disposition of loans designated for exit. Total outstandings and exposure designated for exit during 1999 totaled $3.7 billion and $10.5 billion respectively. As of December 31, 2000, total outstandings associated with this initiative were $1 billion of which $286 million were classified as loans held for sale, with the remainder included in loans. Total exposure related to this initiative was $2.7 billion at December 31, 2000.

What was designated for exit, and when? What initiative does this refer to? Because the total exposure ($2.7 billion) exceeded the total loans for sale on the balance sheet by more than $1 billion, PNC obviously had a lot going on that wasn't appearing on the balance sheet.

Airlines and SPEs

Airlines use off-balance-sheet transactions to finance aircraft purchases. Everyone who follows the industry knows about it, so you should, too.

On its 2001 balance sheet, UAL, the parent company of United, said its long-term debt due within 12 months was $1.2 billion and other long-term debt was $6.6 billion. It also itemized current and future capital lease obligations of $2.2 billion. In the MD&A about capital commitments, the company admitted that it used off-balance-sheet financing for aircraft and facilities acquisitions. It had operating lease commitments of $1.5 billion over the next year and more than $3 billion per year thereafter, for a total of $24 billion. In the footnote to the financial statement about lease commitments, it put a present value on these commitments of $11 billion.

AMR, the parent company of American, also keeps huge aircraft-purchase costs off its balance sheet. Its balance sheet showed total long-term debt of $9 billion and capital lease obligations of $1.7 billion. In the footnote on leases, however, AMR disclosed an additional $17.6 billion in operating lease obligations.

SPEs and extending credit or collateralizing receivables

Nearly every large company, even those you think are in cash businesses, extends credit. Credit, of course, creates collectibility issues and requires reserves. It also raises the possibility that the company has boosted sales primarily by offering easy credit rather than because of genuine demand for its product. Because many companies move some, or even all, of their receivables off the balance sheet, it is impossible to get an accurate picture of the company's true financial condition, unless you understand and can find these off-balance-sheet arrangements.

Department-store chain Target gets most of its revenues from cash purchases or credit cards such as Visa or American Express, where collectibility risks belong to the card issuer, not the retailer. Target issues its own credit card, though, and services the card itself. If customers don't pay the balance, Target loses. Until it reported its fiscal 2001 third-quarter results, Target moved its receivables completely off the balance sheet. It explained this in its 2000 Annual Report, in the MD&A and footnote sections. Still, it changed its policy in the third quarter, so a comparison of the 2000 Form 10-K and the third-quarter Form 10-Q demonstrate how the financial statements changed based on the treatment of these receivables. Although Target claimed it changed the practice because a new accounting rule, SFAS No. 140, changed the definition of an SPE, the company also significantly increased its SPE exposure during the year. In this environment, significantly increasing the use of off-balance-sheet financing would have created credibility problems for Target if it did not improve its disclosure or put the exposure on the balance sheet.

According to Target's 2000 balance sheet, it had long-term debt of $5.6 billion. It did not list any accounts receivable in its assets, but had an entry of "receivable-backed securities" of $1.9 billion. Target packaged all its receivables and transferred them to a special-purpose subsidiary, which sold them (sometimes to the public, sometimes to private investors) as receivable-backed securities. The $1.9 billion on the balance sheet represented only the securities not sold to the public. Target's SPE also had $800 million in securities sold to the public. These securities cost $50 million per year in interest and had to be redeemed five years after they were sold.

This sounds like the equivalent of $800 million more of debt, and $800 million in accounts receivable for which Target did not maintain a reserve. In fact, Target's credit business is a profit center. Target cardholders like to maintain balances, pay high interest rates, and even make late payments (triggering additional revenues for Target). Still, it is a liability that is disclosed in the MD&A and footnotes, but not on the balance sheet itself.

During 2001, Target's SPE doubled the amount of off-balance-sheet receivable-backed securities, selling another $750 million. In putting all the securities on the balance sheet, Target had to make several changes. First, all the old securities, those sold to the public and those sold privately, finally made it onto the balance sheet, as accounts receivable. Second, Target classified the $750 million in new securities as long-term debt.

Using SPEs to hide development expenses

Numerous technology companies use SPEs to fund research and development. This is generally a deceptive tactic, and one that costs companies money to implement. Removing R&D expense from the income statement makes it difficult to determine the company's commitment to research and development, and it keeps investors from seeing how much the company is spending. In addition, some friendly third party usually profits from the arrangement, because the SPE has to have some non-company investors and, if the R&D actually turns something up, the company has to buy the research back, probably at a nice profit to the straw men who put up a little money and let the company call the shots for the SPE.

Cisco Systems, over the previous five years, set up about 15 of these research companies. It funded their development, committed to provide future funding, and had an option (or could be forced) to buy back the companies for Cisco stock. Although Cisco expensed most of the amounts contributed as part of its R&D expense, until it filed its 2002 second-quarter Form 10-Q in March 2002, it never disclosed its future commitments to those enterprises or the cost at which it could or must reacquire the companies. As the Form 10-Q revealed, these contingencies can be expensive. This report was much more detailed than Cisco's previous reports on this subject, and may be a permanent change in the way companies disclose their operations in the wake of Enron.

Commitments to four of those companies (owned by Cisco and its employees in varying percentages) totaled a relatively small amount of its R&D spending. Cisco spent $1.8 billion in R&D over the previous six months (its fiscal year ends on July 31). Over the previous three fiscal years, Cisco had spent $1.66 billion, $2.7 billion, and $3.92 billion on total R&D. For these three start-ups, it spent about $80 million, most of which was included in that R&D spending. It was committed to provide up to $142 million more. Again, this is a drop in the bucket compared to total R&D spending, but Cisco is not the profit juggernaut it used to be or purported to be; that's still a fair chunk of change, and enough of a commitment to deserve disclosure.

More significant is the previously undisclosed cost of buying out the four companies. The three smallest companies, Cisco announced, would be purchased in the next six months for $500 million in Cisco stock. The largest company, if Cisco purchases it, will cost $2.5 billion in stock. That $3 billion expense is huge. It equals a whole year of R&D spending from a company that spends a lot in R&D. Even in Cisco's high-living days, it never had $3 billion in net income in a year. If it kept these assets in plain view, it would probably still have to cough up some stock, part of its compensation plan to keep all these talented researchers on the job. But I can't help think that a large portion of the $3 billion is the cost of keeping these expenses off the balance sheet. Because the investors pay for this dilution, it is a bitter pill to swallow: They have to pay to have the company hide information from them.

The story with all SPEs is basically the same. First, they can be a legitimate way for a company to remove risks to the company. Second, the company frequently retains some risks, so investors need to know about off-balance-sheet transactions. Third, the MD&A and footnotes, to varying degrees, provide information about risks that don't appear on the balance sheet. Fourth, the connection between off-balance-sheet liabilities and Enron's bankruptcy has forced companies to be more forthcoming in those disclosures.

27 Off-Balance-Sheet Liabilities: Synthetic Leases and Dollar General

Conventional operating leases are simple: The company pays rent for a term to the third-party owner. The property is not an asset of the company. Other than current rent payments showing up as expenses on the income statement, the lease has no financial statement impact. (For example, the property is not an asset, future payments are not liabilities, and depreciation of the asset does not appear as an expense.) A synthetic lease looks the same in the financial statements, but has all the tax benefits of ownership. The company sets up an entity to buy or build the property, the entity borrows the purchase price, and the company leases with an obligation to buy the property at the end of the lease.

Synthetic leases have some benefits, but they come with enormous risks. First, the loan for the property is based on the company's credit rating, not just the value of the property. Second, the government allows the company the tax benefits of ownership, even though it is not the title owner. It can deduct payments on the property loan, as well as the depreciation of the property, on its income taxes.

Here is the catch: To get off-balance-sheet treatment, the lease term has to be seven years or less. The company, therefore, is using short-term financing for long-term assets, similar to if you bought your house with the aid of a seven-year rather than 30-year mortgage. If interest rates stay low and property values stay high, no problem. The company can just sell the property at the end of the term to a third party for a profit, or refinance. But what if the company is strapped for cash, or interest rates rise, or property values decline? The company is facing a big credit problem. This is made much worse by the fact that, because this doesn't appear on the balance sheet, you have to be diligent in tracking down this kind of risk.

The details of these arrangements are never clear, but they are usually explained to some degree in the MD&A and the footnote about commitments and contingencies. These explanations are usually distinguished by their incompleteness: credit, loan, or lease arrangements that don't explain who the parties are; an adjective such as "leveraged" in the title of the arrangement; contingencies and rights to purchase or renew but without the terms. (Incidentally, synthetic leases are often used for expensive corporate headquarters. Be suspicious whenever you hear a company is spending a lot on its headquarters. A big office is much more often management's monument to itself than a profit-making business tool.)

Companies make substantial use of the synthetic lease. Apart from its legitimate benefits, it dresses up the financial statement by omitting a large liability. Once you identify a significant lease liability, keep your distance if you can't figure out the terms. Even though synthetic leases are allowed under current accounting rules, which could change, their potential for hiding future risks is substantial.

Dollar General's $500 million hideout

Dollar General, through the late 1990s, had distinguished itself as a top discount retailer in the eastern half of the United States. Central to the strategy, and the success story, was Dollar General's ability to keep costs down through inventory management, favorable lease terms, and other cost-cutting measures.

Retail sales is a low-margin, high-volume business. By the end of 2000, Dollar General operated 5,000 stores, with almost no debt on its balance sheet. Its superior results, it turns out, were accomplished with the benefit of synthetic leases, which, if included in the financial statements, increased debt, expenses, and risk.

For the year ended January 29, 1999, Dollar General reported net income of $182 million on $3.2 billion in sales. Selling, general and administrative expenses, as a percentage of sales, fell for the ninth consecutive year. Long-term debt was a miniscule $786,000. For the year ended January 29, 2000, the company reported net income of $219 million on sales of $3.9 billion. Long-term debt, again, was virtually nonexistent.

In April 2001, Dollar General faced a very bizarre accounting crisis. It had previously replaced Coopers & Lybrand as its auditor with Deloitte & Touche. During 2000, because of the significant accounting issues arising in connection with the audit, the audit committee brought in Arthur Andersen, and Dollar General's finance staff hired KPMG. Deloitte continued as the company's auditor; these additional firms represented just the interests of the audit committee and finance staff. In 2001, PricewaterhouseCoopers (the successor company to Coopers & Lybrand) agreed to replace Deloitte as auditor but resigned six days later because of a conflict of interest. With only five large accounting firms dominating public-company audits, Ernst & Young inevitably entered the picture, becoming the auditor that signed off on the company's 2001 financial statements.

After eight months of evaluation, Dollar General restated its 1998, 1999, and 2000 results, and dramatically recast its balance sheet. Rather than do the same with 1996 and 1997 results, it merely said, "such financial data have not been restated and should not be relied upon." Over the three-year period, the company had to reduce $0.30 of $1.81 in earnings per share, and take another charge of $0.30 per share to settle investor lawsuits. In addition, long-term debt rose by $511 million.

The biggest reason for the restatement was Dollar General's classification of several synthetic leases as operating leases. Instead of reporting these arrangements as leveraged properties owned by the company, it reported them as lease obligations with no ownership consequences. Worse than the restatements, which reflected increased interest expenses, depreciation and amortization costs, and other accounting errors, Dollar General was suddenly a company with huge liabilities in its immediate future. Dollar General had to obtain waivers for violating financial covenants that were conditions to the leases; one lender required a 100 basis-point increase in the interest rate, and the other accelerated the lease term from 2004 to 2002.

The synthetic lease situation was disclosed in several places in the fine print of Dollar General's annual report. The disclosures were specific enough to put investors on notice that the company had big obligations in connection with the leases. For example, in the 1998 Annual Report, the company said in the MD&A that it "has a $225 million leveraged lease facility that funds the construction of new stores, new [Distribution Centers], and a new corporate headquarters. As of January 29, 1999, approximately $143 million of construction costs had been funded under this facility."

The footnote on commitments and contingencies also disclosed the arrangement: "During 1997, the Company entered into a $100 million leveraged lease facility. During 1998, the leveraged lease facility was amended to increase the amount of the facility to $225 million. This facility is being used to fund the construction cost of the Company's corporate headquarters, two distribution centers and a number of store locations." Granted, the disclosure doesn't say anything about what obligations, other than paying rent, the company has under the facility. But if Dollar General is party to the facility, and it is being used to build stores, distribution facilities, and corporate headquarters, the company has some liability here beyond paying rent.

In addition, as is usually the case, cash flow does not lie. The money Dollar General paid in rent appeared as an expense on the income statement. If the company was nothing more than a tenant at all these locations, its property and equipment purchases would be relatively minor, especially for an operation with no long-term debt. In 1998, however, the cash flow statement showed that Dollar General spent $140 million on property and equipment. It reported property and equipment spending of $152 million for 1999. These numbers did not change substantially in the restatement. (Although numerous elements of cash flow changed in the restatement, other than some items being moved around, the results were very similar after reducing the net income.)

28

Pensions

Pension plans are usually the result of agreements (often collective-bargaining agreements) between the company and its workforce to provide certain retirement benefits. Changes in tax laws that encourage employee-retirement savings (Keogh plans, 401(k)s, IRAs, SEPs, etc.) have prompted newer companies to replace pension plans with these employee-participatory plans. Traditional pension plans are still around, though, and, particularly for the large, older companies that have had them for decades, they control gigantic amounts of assets.

If you want a detailed understanding of corporate pension plans, look elsewhere. But here is the short version: The company is obligated to make certain future payments to retirees. It has to contribute to a fund controlled by a trustee enough money to pay these obligations. The reason you don't hear about many unemployed actuaries is because the process of determining how much these obligations will be and how much money the company needs to contribute so that the plan will have enough to meet those obligations is a complicated process. Understandably, companies want to spend as little as possible to meet these obligations. If the assets exceed the expected benefits to be paid out, the plan is "overfunded" and the company doesn't have to add to it. If the expected benefits to be paid exceed the assets, the plan is "underfunded" and the company has to put in some money.

In periods of financial decline, as we've had in 2000 and 2001, the assets in these pension plans are actually losing money. You need to read the balance sheet and the footnote on employee benefit plans to see if the plan has become underfunded and the size of the obligation the company has to fund the plan.

Over the last several years, companies faced the opposite problem. When the stock market was going gangbusters, pension plan assets grew much faster than benefits paid, and many plans became significantly overfunded. Practically speaking, the biggest benefit a company can get from an overfunded pension plan is not having to make contributions to the plan. Because a trustee controls the assets, the company can't withdraw any surplus. Nevertheless, current accounting rules allow companies to include returns on assets in excess of benefits paid as net income. (It usually shows up as a reduction in costs or SG&A.) In addition, because of all the assumptions that go into figuring out obligations and returns, a company, by altering its assumed rate of return, can increase the contribution of the pension plan to net income.

General Electric

If you look on General Electric's income statement for the contribution made by its overfunded pension plan, you won't find it. Even with the expanded disclosures in its 2001 Annual Report, the $1.48 billion earned by the plan's assets, above all costs and obligations, does not appear as a separate item, nor is there a reference to the pension footnote.

GE has a huge, undefined item in its income statement called "other costs and expenses." For 2001, other costs and expenses were $28.1 billion. Because GE does not have an SG&A line on the income statement, this must be where it recognizes all costs not directly related to producing goods and services. Because the pension footnote referred to the pension gain as "net cost reductions from post-retirement benefit plans,"

GE took the $1.48 billion as a reduction in cost rather than as a form of revenue. It's good to know that GE's pension plan is doing so well that it won't have to contribute to it for awhile, but that reduction in cost amounted to more than 10 percent of GE's $13.7 billion in net income for 2001.

There is also some question about whether the pension plan really performed that well in 2001. According to the pension footnote, the fair value of plan assets at the beginning of 2001 was $49.7 billion. It paid $2 billion in benefits during the year, and actually lost $2.8 billion on pension investments. (This latter amount is not surprising, considering how much everyone who invested lost during 2001.) The fair value of the assets at the end of the year was $45 billion, a reduction of $4.7 billion in value.

GE was able to squeeze earnings (in the form of cost reductions) from its pension plan during a bad investment year because of the use of actuarial assumptions. (SFAS No. 87, adopted by the FASB during the 1980s, allows the use of actuarial assumptions, including assumptions on returns, to smooth out year-to-year returns on plan assets.) Figuring out how much benefit payments will be and how assets will perform into the indefinite future is the work of actuaries, and the numbers are dictated more by the assumptions than the actual returns for a particular year. During 2001, GE assumed a return on assets of 9.5 percent. This is similar to what other companies assumed for their pension assets, but it is much more than actual returns. As assets shrink from poor actual returns, companies have to change the assumptions, but they get the income boost in the meantime for maintaining unrealistic assumptions. GE is reducing its return on assets for 2002 to 8.5 percent. That means its return of assets will be 1 percent less than in 2001. With $45 billion in total pension assets, that will mean a hit to GE's net income of $450 million.

Verizon

Verizon, the modern incarnation of Bell Atlantic, NYNEX, and GTE, has one of the biggest and oldest pension plans in the United States. Especially with its core telecommunications business suffering along with the rest of that industry, the returns on its pension plan assets have artificially boosted the bottom line even more than GE achieved with its pension plan.

Verizon is one of those companies for which you must read the financial statements closely to figure out what's going on. It expertly spins its results, so you will be lost if you accept its characterizations or rely on a news report. Verizon reported "adjusted" earnings per share of $3 in 2001. Based on GAAP EPS, however, it earned just $0.14. So which is it, the $389 million according to GAAP or the $8.2 billion according to Verizon's pro forma reporting? You can judge for yourself, but only if you read the financial statements. Verizon adjusted out the following: $4.8 billion on losses in value of securities, $1 billion in severance and retirement costs, $663 million in international restructuring, $600 million in transition costs, and $226 million from asset sales.

In contrast, Verizon did not adjust out the favorable impact of the gains in its pension assets, even though the company could not access those gains. Here is the impact of Verizon's total benefit income, along with net income, in which those gains are included (amounts in millions):

	2001	2000	1999
Total benefit income	$1,848	$3,489	$1,925
Net income	389	11,787	8,260

As you can see, pension gains added a significant amount to Verizon's net income in 1999 and 2000, and kept it from reporting a significant loss in 2001.

Verizon assumed a slightly lower level of return on assets than GE, 9.25 percent. On the other hand, the expected return on assets for 2001 was $4.8 billion. The actual return was a loss of $3 billion. Along with the payment of benefits during the year, the surplus in the plan fell from $12.1 billion to $8.2 billion.

Qwest

Qwest has several pension and post-retirement plans. Its pension plan is overfunded, but the company is, as of December 31, 2001, expected to owe retirees nearly $3 billion more than the current value of post-retirement healthcare and life-insurance plans. On the balance sheet, Qwest lists as a liability "post-retirement and other post-employment benefit obligations" in 2001 of $2.973 billion. (This obligation was $2.952 billion in 2000.)

In Qwest's employee benefits footnote, it provides information about the status and future impact of its pension and other post-retirement plans. As nearly all companies do, it elected long ago to recognize actual returns on pension and retirement assets over a five-year period when computing the market value of plan assets. Qwest explained, "This method has the effect of smoothing market volatility that may be experienced from year to year." This "smoothing" can delay recognition of significant gains as actual returns improve, but it also delays recognition of losses when returns decline.

Qwest separated the numbers for its pension and post-retirement plans, and provided tables calculating benefit obligations, the fair value of plans, the funded status of the plans, and the actuarial assumptions of the plans. Combining information from those tables, you can see on page 202 the details behind this liability.

From Qwest's 2001 employee benefit footnote
Post-retirement plans
(amounts in millions)

	12/31/01	12/31/00
Benefit obligation accrued at beginning of year	$4,500	$4,344
Benefit obligation accrued at year end	4,700	4,500
Fair value of plan assets at beginning of year	2,407	2,886
Fair value of plan assets at year end	2,045	2,407
Prepaid benefit (accrued cost)	(2,840)	(2,881)

Qwest hasn't exactly been rushing to make up that deficit. In the footnote, it said that it contributed $16 million to the post-retirement plans in 2000 and $18 million in 1999. It didn't make any contribution in 2001. It's going to have to pay that money sometime, so you need to factor that into any evaluation of a company with a deficit in any of its benefit plans.

29

Enron in 5 Minutes

Didn't anyone find it strange that even the so-called experts didn't have any idea how Enron made money? Or even stranger, that they still recommended buying the stock despite that? In the investment world, ignorance is bliss, but only for a little while. David Fleischer, a stock analyst at Goldman Sachs, recommended Enron stock and said in early 2001 that "Enron has built unique and, in our view, extraordinary franchises in several business units in very large markets." At the same time, he admitted that it was difficult to analyze Enron "with as little information as we have." The Chief Financial Officer, Andrew Fastow, admitted to *Fortune* that there were parts of the operation they didn't want people to understand: "We don't want to tell anyone where we're making money." If the smartest people in the investing world bought into that, they couldn't have been all that smart.

Of course, thousands of individual investors and employees got burned on the same stock. Could that have been different? What could individual investors have noticed if the employees and the institutions were pouring money in? Even with fraud and doctoring the numbers, there were many scary things about Enron's financial statements. All investors had to do was read them.

1. Enron sure didn't look like a growth company.

For a growth company with an accelerating stock, Enron's net income wasn't growing very fast. Net income is the easiest number to manipulate and investors pay too much attention to it (and its twin, earnings per share). At a minimum, if you are going to pay a growth-multiple for earnings, the company should at least give you rapid earnings growth.

Enron Corp. (years ended December 31)

Year	Net Income (millions)	EPS
1998	$666	$1.01
1999	827	1.10
2000	896	1.12

2. Enron's operating cash flow looked pretty, but stunk.

In the Introduction, I described the warning signs about Enron's operating cash flow.

3. Increased receivables and payables are a red flag.

Even if these things didn't gum up Enron's cash flow, you should be wary of any company that looks as if it is getting behind in collecting, and paying, its bills.

From Enron's Balance Sheet (amounts in millions)

	2000	1999
Net trade receivables	$10,396	3,030
Other receivables	1,874	518
Inventories	953	598
Deposits	2,433	81
Other current assets	1,333	535
Accounts payable	9,777	2,154
Other current liabilities	2,178	1,724

4. Understanding Enron's "merchant" and "price risk activities" is an exercise in futility.

In the MD&A section describing its capital structure, Enron disclosed that it entered into certain financial contracts "which contain provisions for early settlement in the event of a significant market price decline in which Enron's common stock falls below certain levels (prices ranging from $28.20 to $55 per share) or if the credit ratings for Enron's unsecured, senior long-term debt obligations fall below investment grade." Maybe some of this is best understood in hindsight, but the worst kind of risk a company can face is one triggered by its stock price or debt rating. Think about it: If things are going bad, the stock price could fall or the credit-rating agencies could lower their credit ratings. If the company just had the kind of problems that cut its stock price and credit rating, it can't possibly be in a situation where it can satisfy a bunch of creditors, partners, and counter-parties demanding to be paid immediately.

How about this for a gigantic and unknowable uncertainty? In Footnote 3 to the financial statements, the footnote about "price risk management activities and financial instruments," Enron cautioned that the notional amounts of the contracts, disclosed in the footnote, have nothing to do with the assets and liabilities, or gains and losses for the future. "[N]otional amounts do not accurately measure Enron's exposure to market or credit risks. The maximum terms in years detailed above are not indicative of likely future cash flows as these positions may be offset in the markets at any time in response to the company's price risk management needs to the extent available in the market."

5. The scope of Enron's "unconsolidated equity affiliates" automatically created an unacceptable level of risk.

Footnote 9 described Enron's unconsolidated joint affiliates. Enron admitted to investments in unconsolidated joint affiliates valued at $5.3 billion. Included in that latter figure were nine enterprises and "other," which accounted for $1.6 billion of the total.

Enron put together a crazy little balance sheet and income statement for this mysterious conglomeration of off-balance-sheet investments. There are lots of assets, but there is no clue what they consist of, except for a note saying that $410 million of them are notes receivable from Enron. There are also current liabilities of $4.7 billion, long-term debt of $9.7 billion, and other non-current liabilities of $6.1 billion. These are pretty substantial numbers. Enron's balance sheet contained $8.5 billion of long-term debt. Why would you want to invest in a company that explained in detail—amounts, dates, interest rates—its $8.5 billion in long-term debt, then told you there was another $9.7 billion out there owed by some affiliated entity, but won't disclose who else owns the entity, its creditworthiness, the apportionment of risk between Enron and the other investors, or any details about the terms of the debt?

Footnote 16, "related party transactions," is also a piece of work. It described seven different transactions with a certain related party operated by "a senior officer of Enron." That was CFO Andrew Fastow, but Enron couldn't bring itself to tell you. A couple of the transactions involved investments in the billions of dollars.

6. In August 2001, Enron issued an ugly second-quarter report.

In the Introduction, I described Enron's negative operating cash flow in its last pre-bankruptcy quarterly report.

Some of these matters are definitely easier to spot after the fact. But the real problem was that no one was looking. (Bethany McLean, an excellent financial reporter at *Fortune*, blew the whistle on these guys back in March 2001, six months before the company admitted any trouble. Few investors took notice at the time.) It looks like there was a lot of wrongdoing at Enron. The headlines in early 2002 tell the story: Off-balance-sheet risks totaling billions, misclassifying assets in the billions, destruction of documents, insider selling, the suicide of the former vice chairman. You wouldn't know these things until afterward, but with a whole world to invest in, could someone honestly read these financial statements and conclude this was the best opportunity available?

30

Cash Flow

It should be clear if you have gotten this far that I consider the information in the cash flow statement, especially operating cash flow, to be the best information available on how the company is really performing.

I read recently that over the life of a company, cash flow and net income will be the same. I hadn't thought of it that way but it's true. If a company starts and ends with nothing, however profitable or unprofitable it is in between, the net income and cash flow over the life of the company will work out to the same number. All cash flow really does, then, is compensate for the weaknesses of accrual accounting. Most accounting scams, or merely aggressive uses of the rules, involve non-cash transactions; cash is too difficult to fake, unless you can convincingly print it in your basement. The cash flow statement factors out those non-cash transactions. Cash flow is about what a company spends and receives, not about how or when it recognizes it.

In many of the big accounting errors and frauds of the past several years, subsequent restatements of results have had little effect on the cash flow statement. For example, look at the restatement of MicroStrategy, the result of conduct described in Chapter 13. Among the restatements MicroStrategy made, it restated first- and second-quarter 1999 results, reducing revenue by $12 million and net income by $5 million.

MicroStrategy Income Statement, first six months, 1999 (abridged) (amounts in thousands)

January-June 1999	Original	Restated
Total revenues	$81,422	$69,787
Total cost of revenues	15,598	15,598
Total operating expenses	58,710	58,710
Net income	5,070	(3,807)

Look at MicroStrategy's operating cash flow from the same six months. It was actually restated upward, and the difference between the original cash flow and the restatement was less than $100,000.

MicroStrategy Operating Cash Flow, first six months, 1999 (abridged) (amounts in thousands)

	Original	Restated
Net income	$5,070	$(3,807)
Adjustments to reconcile net income to net cash		
Depreciation and amortization	2,771	2,855
Provision for doubtful accounts	773	773
Amortization of deferred compensation	150	150
Changes in operating assets and liabilities		
Accounts receivable	(14,786)	(2,236)
Prepaid expenses and other current assets	(1,954)	(1,454)
Accounts payable and accrued expenses	2,457	(285)
Deferred revenue	4,072	3,558
Deposits and other assets	(85)	(85)
Long-term accounts receivable	900	0
Net cash used in operations	(632)	(547)

This is generally the case. Even when the restatement is of a much larger magnitude, such as the $1.5 billion net income restatement over five years by Waste Management, operating cash flow changed by a relatively small amount.

Even when the problem is merely aggressive accounting, or investors getting more excited than the results justify, the operating cash flow can signal an underlying weakness in the business before the earnings number tips off everyone. Many stock plunges are preceded by a period where earnings are still rising and investors are still flocking to the stock, but the cash flow is disintegrating, or at least giving signals that trouble is on the horizon.

When Sun Microsystems issued its earnings release for the first quarter of 2001 in October 2000 (Sun's fiscal year starts July 1), things were going great. Revenues were $5 billion, 60 percent more than the year-earlier period. Net income was $510 million, up 85 percent over the same quarter the year before. It seemed like the party was going to continue; orders for the quarter increased 54 percent over the first quarter of 1999. Sun's stock soon reached its all-time high of $60 per share, a six-fold increase in less than two years.

By March 2001, however, the earnings increases stopped, the hard times began, and the stock dropped to $20 per share. A year later, it was at half that price. Who would have known?

The seeds of Sun's problems appeared in its cash flow statement. (Incidentally, companies can choose whether or not they want to include a cash flow statement with their earnings press release; Sun declined.)

Sun Microsystems, Operating Cash Flow, 1ˢᵗ Quarter 2001 (amounts in millions)

Net income	$510
Adjustments to reconcile net income to net cash	
Depreciation and amortization	208
Tax benefits from employee stock plans	472
Changes in accounts receivable	(266)
Changes in inventory	(118)
Changes in other current and long-term assets	(154)
Changes in accounts payable	219
Changes in other current and long-term liabilities	(170)
Net cash provided by operating activities	710

It looks like good cash flow, significantly above net income and much more than the $391 million of the year-earlier quarter. Sun's operating cash flow demonstrates everything that can be misleading about a cash flow statement. None of this is fabricated; you just have to understand its implications.

Sun's tax benefit from employee stock plans of $472 million is a number you should discount or ignore. It is a real number—Sun gets a tax benefit of that size—but it's not traditional "operating" cash flow and it is purely speculative whether this can continue. As was stated in Chapter 22 about stock options, companies receive a tax deduction for the value of stock options, an amount that depends significantly on the market price of the stock. A high stock price means a high deduction, so all you're really doing when you count a big options-related tax benefit as part of cash flow is recognizing that the company's stock price went up a lot. That's not a reason to buy a stock; it's probably a reason to avoid it.

Another favorable item investors should discount is an increase in accounts payable. Sun's operating cash flow improved by $219 million because of this. As I have said frequently, owing more money without paying it helps only in the short term.

Every other aspect of operating cash flow was negative. Inventory and accounts receivable rose, reducing cash flow by $384 million for the quarter. You don't even have to figure out the source of the additional $324 million in reductions in operating cash flow. Whatever the reason, it just made a bad situation worse.

Obviously, it's easier to make these observations after everyone has soured on the stock. It would be difficult to pull the trigger and sell such a successful stock, especially when it appeared earnings and cash flow were still improving. But what about all the people who decided to buy in at $60 per share? After that gigantic run-up and the huge price-earnings multiple, they should have looked for something to suggest that the run would continue. Instead, they would have found that, without several items likely not to continue, operating cash flow was dismal.

Make sure you look at the real article and not someone else's analysis of cash flow. You will hear about other measures, including **free cash flow** or **EBITDA**. Free cash flow usually refers to cash flow from operations after capital expenditures. There is no standard definition, though, and several of the standard items in operating cash flow should be considered differently than others. EBITDA, Earnings Before Interest, Taxes, Depreciation, and Amortization, isn't cash flow at all. It includes just about every manipulation of earnings, including those connected with revenue recognition. Neglecting interest payments, or any aspect of a company's debt, is also a dangerous exercise.

The message of this book applies to cash flow more than anything else: Read the financial statements for yourself. It's not that difficult.

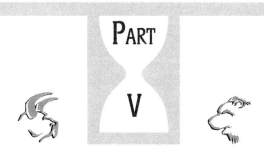

PART V

One More
5 Minute Shot

Just as we did with IBM in Chapters 4 and 5, let's pick up the financial statements of a well-known, complex corporation and see what we can learn from a quick reading. With the familiarity we have developed through the first 30 chapters, you should no longer be intimidated by the prospect and should have many ways of evaluating a modern public company.

If you plan to plunk down some serious money in the stock market, you should think about taking more than five minutes studying financial reports, although these are the techniques you should still use. In addition, there is no substitute for a strong understanding of the company's business. The financial statements will tell you how the company performed and how much credibility you should give to the company's predictions of how it will perform, but they can't tell you about changing demand in the company's business, competitive pressures, or other events outside past financial performance that bear on the future. Finally, plenty will change between when I write this and when you read it. I include this next chapter, which might take a little more than five minutes to read, to help get you started developing your skills as a financial-statement detective. You have to do the actual work with the most recently available information when it comes time to make your investing decisions.

5 Minutes With AOL Time Warner (Okay, Maybe 10)

31

No one can predict what the situation will be by the time you read this, but as I write it, AOL Time Warner is facing a major crisis of confidence among investors. The merger between AOL and Time Warner is being hailed as one of the worst business decisions ever. Forget about the lofty heights of AOL stock during the dot-com boom, or Time Warner's stock performance during the late 1990s. The day these companies completed their merger in January 2001, after all the air had been let out of Internet stocks and the giddy atmosphere of a big deal had passed, the combined company's stock price was $48 per share. Fifteen months later, just a few weeks after issuing its 2001 Annual Report, AOL Time Warner's stock traded below $20 per share. Some of the big institutional investors—the "smart money"—appear to be racing to distance themselves from this stock. (For shorthand purposes, I'm going to call the combined company "AOL." It was designated the successor company, but in fact, the online business is just another subsidiary of the pre-existing media conglomerate of pre-merger Time Warner.)

If you content yourself with the headlines, you can choose from AOL's positive spin, or the negative impression most commentators in print, on TV, and over the Internet have been providing. As I mentioned in Chapter 21 about pro forma reporting, AOL thought it was a great year, all things considered.

Revenues rose 6 percent, normalized free cash flow rose 238 percent, EBITDA grew 14 percent. You could instead believe the news reports going the other way: Advertising revenue, which drives most of the company's operations, was awful and will continue to be awful, and the company had a net loss of $4.9 billion.

Or you can take a third route and read the report for yourself. (I encourage you, at some point while reading this chapter, to get the 2001 Annual Report. It is available online, at www.*aoltimewarner.com/investors/annual_reports/pdf/ 2001ar.pdf.*)

MD&A

Use of EBITDA.

AOL provided its justification for including EBITDA in its evaluation of operations:

> AOL Time Warner considers EBITDA an important indicator of the operational strength and performance of its businesses, including the ability to provide cash flows to service debt and fund capital expenditures. In addition, EBITDA eliminates the uneven effect across all business segments of considerable amounts of noncash depreciation of tangible assets and amortization of goodwill and intangible assets recognized in business combinations accounted for by the purchase method.

This is a good explanation, although this same explanation better supports ignoring EPS and EBITDA and doing your own analysis, taking some elements of both, along with some elements both ignore, such as the composition of AOL's debt and its capital spending requirements. AOL's explanation ended with a proper caveat: "EBITDA should be considered in addition to, not as a substitute for, operating income (loss), net income (loss), and other measures of financial performance reported in accordance with generally accepted accounting principles." Actually, they have to say that, but it's good advice. In fact, if you've gotten far enough to read it, there's a good chance you're well on the way to doing your own evaluation.

Transactions affecting comparability

This is another section where AOL made its pitch about how pro forma reporting is better than GAAP reporting. The good thing about these presentations is that the company gives you more information, and categorizes it for you, in ways you may not learn about if you read only the financial statements themselves. For example, AOL had $250 million in merger costs in 2001. I don't think you should disregard that. If this company rebounds, it will continue wheeling and dealing, and those kinds of costs will continue. And if it fails to rebound, it's going to start selling, spinning off, and otherwise shedding some operations; transaction costs will continue in that form.

AOL also mentioned that it took "non-cash pretax charges" of $2.5 billion to reduce the carrying value of certain investments. Half of this was to mark down the value of 44-percent-owned Time Warner Telecom Inc. As we discussed in Chapter 18–20, this meant that AOL did not have to shell out that amount in 2001, but it still had an impact worth considering. We need to investigate, in our analysis of these financial statements, why it took the write-down. Most likely, its cash flow analysis indicated that it would not recoup the carrying value, which was probably its cost. For a company with $22 billion in debt, a declaration that a certain group of assets won't generate enough cash to pay for themselves can be significant. If you carefully consider AOL's ability to service its debt, you don't have to concern yourself with the write-down, but at least use this as a warning that its ability to service that debt is impaired, by its own admission.

This whole section of the MD&A is a good overview of all the "non-operating" or "one-time" elements affecting AOL's financial statements.

Consolidated results

There are so many comparability issues that it is hard to make a quick review of management's narrative of how business fared in 2001. It is, however, worthwhile to try. AOL has six business segments: its online service, cable, filmed entertainment, networks, music, and publishing.

➤ Online revenue grew from $7.7 billion to $8.7 billion, with consistent increases in subscription revenues, advertising, and content. The driving force is the AOL service, and it did well, increasing subscribers and increasing prices by $1.95 per month. If you own a computer, you have to evaluate how long this can continue. AOL is a premium-priced service and some of its growth depends on charging a premium price. With more people getting their access elsewhere, especially when they switch to broadband service from dial-up service, will AOL continue to have its hold on the market and be able to increase prices? (It helps the company that its cable segment can hold on to many of those broadband seekers.) Advertising revenues improved in part because of contracts AOL negotiated in prior years and recorded as revenue during 2001. With the bad advertising market, this becomes a problem in the near-term future, completely reversing the 1999 impression of AOL that its development of online advertising revenue would be its best route to success.

➤ Cable revenue grew from $6 billion to $7 billion, in part by signing up subscribers to high-speed online services. This should continue to improve over the next several years.

➤ Filmed entertainment had a good year, increasing from $8.1 billion to $8.7 billion. It made a bunch of money off the syndication of *Friends* and *Seinfeld*; you need to know more information than presented here to decide if that can continue. It also scored big with *Harry Potter* and

Lord of the Rings, two movie franchises that could produce lots of sequels and ancillary revenue. The shift from videocassettes to DVDs also improved revenues.

➤ Network revenue increased slightly, from $6.8 billion to $7 billion. Subscription revenue increased but ad revenue was mixed among different networks. The reliance on advertising revenue could be a problem in the future.

➤ Music has become a weakness for AOL. Revenues declined from $4.1 billion to $3.9 billion. The company blamed changes in currency exchange rates and lower industry-wide sales, plus higher marketing and promotion costs. I'm not in a position to say, but maybe the problem is with the quality of its artists. In this bad advertising market, which hurts AOL in so many ways, it seems like it would be cheaper to market and promote artists. Plus, AOL controls so many media outlets that, if it's taking a bath on advertising revenue, it should devote some of that space to advertising its own products.

➤ Publishing revenues increased slightly from $4.6 billion to $4.8 billion. Some of the increase came from the acquisition of Times Mirror's magazine group at the end of 2000, and the advertising market held down revenues.

Financial condition and liquidity

AOL's operating cash flow was $5.3 billion. Its EBITDA was $9.6 billion. The difference was payments of $1.2 billion in interest, $340 million in taxes, $1.4 billion in payments to settle restructuring and merger liabilities, and $1.4 billion in working capital requirements. That's a good nutshell reason why you're better off looking at cash flow than EBITDA.

EBITDA also fails to include items from investing cash flow. For AOL, that included $4.1 billion used for acquisitions; $3.6 billion in capital expenditures and product development costs, which will become the depreciation and amortization charges of future years; and $2.5 billion received in cash from mergers and proceeds from sales of investments. The largest portion of AOL's capital spending was on its cable systems, part of a long-term effort to upgrade them and provide more services. That cost $2.2 billion in 2001, a slight increase from 2000, and is an essential part of any analysis of the future of the company.

AOL's financing activities included spending $3 billion to purchase its own shares, $926 million received from the exercise of employee stock options, and $792 million in net new debt.

Off-balance-sheet obligations

AOL has significant commitments, both expected and contingent, which do not appear on its balance sheet. In addition to certain disclosures in the footnotes, the MD&A provides a detailed summary. It has used SPEs to obtain $1.9 billion in debt by securitizing receivables and backlog, and through real estate and aircraft operating leases. It has an additional $500 million in capacity for further borrowing through SPEs. The company insisted "there would be no claims on the Company for the receivables or backlog contracts previously sold."

AOL also entered into a total of $28 billion in firm commitments, securing future rights to assets and services, in exchange for future payments. These do not show up on the balance sheet. The largest commitment, to pay $7 billion to Bertelsmann for its ownership of AOL Europe, is due during 2002. Another $5 billion in commitments are due during 2002, including production deals, payments to network providers, operating leases, and obligations to actors, authors, athletes, and so on. Another $8.5 billion is due in 2003 through 2005, and $7.5 billion is due in 2006 and thereafter.

Finally, AOL has $3.5 billion in contingent commitments, mostly consisting of guarantees to joint venture partners under leases. Most of these commitments don't expire for more than five years.

Accounting policies

AOL enters into multiple-element contracts that require, under SAB 101, apportioning the revenue over the life of the contract. AOL, because it's in the movie business, devotes a few paragraphs to recognition of film costs and revenues. Frankly, one of the best things about movie companies becoming entertainment conglomerates is that they have outgrown receiving significant portion of revenues from movies, or paying a significant portion of expenses to make movies. Movie accounting is a hornet's nest, requiring estimates during the production process of the total expected revenue over the life of the film, up-front payment of expenses but amortization over the life of the film, and periodic impairment charges whenever the company determines it will not recover its costs.

Financial statements

Consolidated statement of operations

As the MD&A summarized, most of AOL's comparisons between 2000 and 2001 were decent. Overall advertising revenue fell from $8.7 billion to $8.4 billion, and that probably understated the future dimension of the problem. Amortization of goodwill and intangibles totaled $7.2 billion. Considering the economic conditions of 2001, AOL's business held together well, except for "other income (expense)." A $1.3 billion expense in 2001, it ballooned to $3.5 billion. In the MD&A, the company said this was primarily because of the charges to reduce the carrying value of Time Warner Telecom and other investments.

Consolidated balance sheet

Receivables stayed steady at $6 billion, less an allowance of $1.9 billion. (In 2000, the allowance was $1.7 billion.) Kudos to the company for increasing the receivable; so many companies cut the receivable during bad times to boost results. AOL had $128 billion in goodwill on the balance sheet, largely the result of the merger, plus both companies' past dealing ways. AOL announced in January 2002, and the annual report makes reference to it, that it will take an impairment charge sometime in 2002 of $54 billion of that goodwill. The company had $22.8 billion in long-term debt, but only $48 million of it due in 2002.

Consolidated statement of cash flows

This is where you really have to get a handle on what kind of company AOL is. It's clear that earnings won't tell you; the company had too many other charges and expenses that obscure operations. EBITDA isn't good enough either; it omitted plenty of important information on costs going forward.

An abridged version of AOL's cash flow statement is shown on page 223. I have eliminated entries that are relatively small, but the totals include those numbers.

We discussed what most of these items represented in the MD&A, so there isn't much new here. Operating cash flow looks very strong. Despite having a giant debt load and a bad operating environment, the company continued to go acquisition-crazy, spending more on acquisitions than on capital expenditures for the assets it already had. (That's apparently not changing, with the early 2002 announcement that AOL was acquiring AOL Europe from Bertelsmann.)

Footnotes

One of the virtues of going through the annual report in detail is that you can read different explanations of the same material. By reviewing the MD&A so carefully, we can give less emphasis to many items described in the footnotes: description of individual segments, SPE, pro forma measures, and elements of various charges.

AOL Time Warner's Cash Flow Statement (abridged)
(amounts in millions)

	2001 historical	2000 pro forma
OPERATING ACTIVITIES		
Net income (loss)	$(4,921)	$(4,370)
Depreciation & amortization	9,203	8,650
Amortization of film costs	2,380	2,032
Loss on write-down of investments	2,537	517
Equity losses of other investee companies after distributions	975	1,224
Changes in receivables	(484)	(924)
Changes in inventories	(2,801)	(2,291)
Changes in accounts payable and other liabilities	(1,952)	1,259
Other balance sheet changes	391	(1,373)
Cash provided by operating activities	5,294	4,644
INVESTING ACTIVITIES		
Investments & acquisitions	(4,177)	(3,758)
Capital expenditures & product development costs	(3,634)	(3,560)
Investment proceeds	1,851	1,431
Cash used by investing activities	(5,270)	(5,889)
FINANCING ACTIVIITES		
Borrowings	10,692	4,660
Debt repayments	(9,900)	(3,043)
Proceeds from exercise of stock options	926	704
Repurchases of common stock	(3,031)	(65)
Cash provided (used) by financing activities	(1,915)	707
INCREASE (DECREASE) IN CASH AND EQUIVALENTS	(1,891)	(538)

Accounting policies

This footnote provided AOL's amortization schedules for intangible assets, although this will be different in the future for some of the items after the adoption of SFAS No. 142. AOL also explained how it put together the 2000 pro forma results for the combined company. Without some kind of combination of prior AOL and Time Warner results, it would be impossible to compare 2001 results against any prior time period, so the pro forma presentation is helpful, and this footnote explanation will allow you to determine if AOL combined the results in a reasonable way. This footnote also provided a detailed explanation of each division's policy for recognizing revenues and costs.

A significant amount of AOL's assets were owned in partnerships with other entities. If AOL had a controlling interest, it reported 100 percent of the results in its financial statements, then separately subtracted "minority interest." If it had a significant interest but not control (even sometimes when it owned more than 50 percent but its partners had rights enabling them to influence day-to-day operations), it accounted for these assets using the **equity method**. Under this method, only AOL's investment in and amounts due to and from the operations were included in the balance sheet, only its share of the earnings was included in the income statement, and only dividends, cash distributions, loans or other cash received, additional cash investments, loan repayments, or other cash paid, were included in the cash flow statement. Where AOL did not have a controlling interest or significant influence, it accounted for the investment at cost, unless it could trade its interest in a public market without restrictions, in which case it accounted for the investment at market value.

Merger-related costs

For a wheeling-dealing kind of company such as AOL, these costs were individually one-time events, but in aggregate they are a way of life. AOL took $1.3 billion in restructuring charges during 2001 to exit certain businesses and terminate employees. This was added to the goodwill recorded in connection with the merger. The footnote showed how the company paid out $465 million and estimated another $875 million in current liabilities. (Consider this a cost of doing business. Not only will AOL always have merger-related costs, but some of these, like the cost to exit World Championship Wrestling operations, are part of the daily business of an entertainment company that develops programming. When it fails and costs money, that's an operating cost. It was a coincidence that AOL exited the operation following a merger.)

Partnerships

AOL (primarily through prior arrangements of Time Warner) owned two-thirds of certain cable assets with Advance/Newhouse. In the financial statements, the entire results were included, with a line entry subtracting the minority interest. The footnote discussed the possibility that Advance/Newhouse would withdraw from the partnership, and the consequences thereof. AOL had a similar deal with AT&T, covering Road Runner, a high-speed online business (in which Advance/Newhouse, Compaq, and Microsoft were along for the ride). AOL owned 44 percent of Time Warner Telecom with the remainder owned by AT&T, Advance/Newhouse, and other investors. AOL was partnered with Bertelsmann in AOL Europe, an arrangement where Bertelsmann forced AOL to buy it out in early 2002 for $7 billion.

The most sprawling of AOL's partnership interests was with AT&T, Time Warner Entertainment. In 1992, Time Warner spun off significant assets—the filmed entertainment, networks, and cable businesses it owned at the time—in exchange for an investment by AT&T. AOL owned 75 percent of the venture, AT&T the other 25 percent. That ownership may also currently be in flux.

Investments

AOL explained the ownership structure of numerous investments (including Time Warner Telecom, Courtroom Television Network, and Comedy Central) that it accounted for on an equity basis. The footnote provided limited financial information and the financial-statement impact of these investments.

Debt

AOL had a lot of debt, most of it at low interest rates. One of the overlooked consequences of the state of affairs in 2001 and 2002 is that this has been a great time for companies to owe money. AOL paid 3-percent interest on its $5 billion in commercial paper and 6.9-percent interest on its $17 billion in fixed-rate public debt. This footnote also explained the company's use of SPEs. This explanation is similar to that provided in the MD&A, although it is more detailed. I consider a negative when a company builds itself elaborate headquarters, which AOL is using an SPE to do at Columbus Circle in New York City. Relatively speaking, the SPEs created to securitize receivables and backlog don't put AOL at much risk, but the SPEs building corporate headquarters in New York and new facilities for Turner in Atlanta include guarantees by AOL.

Taxes

The company had $12 billion in net operating losses, which is a nice thing to have.

Stock options

Time Warner has traditionally been a company that lards its employees (especially the ones at the top) with stock options. If stock options had been included as part of compensation costs, the company would have lost an additional $1.4 billion. As of December 31, 2001, the company had options to acquire 627 million shares outstanding, with a weighted-average exercise price of $31.88. I would watch to see if AOL reprices some of those options, a common move when a company's stock price dives, but inconsistent with the idea that options are supposed to provide an incentive for employees to improve the company.

Commitments and contingencies

AOL's rent expense was about $1 billion per year. It also had, as explained in the MD&A, about $26 billion in firm and contingent commitments.

The decision whether to invest in AOL Time Warner is a complicated one. However, it can be made on an informed basis if you take the time to review the financial information. If you bypass the rhetoric in the press releases and news stories, understanding the company is not beyond your ability. Despite the difficult advertising market, the company's subscription-based revenues rose, and constitute a significant portion of the total. The movie business did well and has prospects to continue doing well. The company conservatively reserves for uncollectible receivables. Cash flow was quite strong, but the company spent (and will probably continue to spend) significant dollars to acquire more assets.

AOL Time Warner is also a model for understanding such things as "pro form results" and EBITDA. In this company, pro forma reporting was valuable, because it would otherwise be impossible to compare the recent consolidated results with prior AOL-only results. EBITDA, on the other hand, is inferior to cash flow and you rely on it at your peril.

Fear of Financial Statements

Was that all so difficult? Maybe some of the chapters took longer than five minutes, and maybe you have to reread a few to really understand it all. But the important thing is that there are simple techniques out there: comparing operating cash flow to net income, checking the rise in receivables and inventories against the rise in revenues, checking the footnotes for the details on restructuring and other one-time charges, and looking at the MD&A and the footnotes for the off-balance-sheet risks.

More importantly, I hope I took some of the fear out of reading a company's financial statements. The biggest scams perpetrated by corporations hide in plain sight. Simply by virtue of investors refusing to educate themselves by reading the financial statements, companies can get away with, if not murder, several other felonies. No one should be afraid, especially you, now that you understand what the terms mean and where to find the most important information.

Enron should be the final wake-up call, but it won't be. Investors have lost huge amounts of money investing in companies that were fraudulent or simply overvalued because their results did not match their stock price. Very few people, it seems, got smarter as a result of frauds involving Sunbeam, Waste Management, or Oxford Health. On the positive side, this means you will have a giant advantage over the people and institutions on the other side of the trade if you take just a little time to learn from those frauds, and from the financial information investors ignored while bidding the stocks of companies such as MicroStrategy, Sun Microsystems, and Lucent into the stratosphere.

I can't promise that your analysis will be right all the time, or that you won't still lose money sometimes when a company turns out to be the opposite of the signals you picked up in your five-minute review. But these techniques will make you a more careful investor and a smarter investor, and that has to make you money in the long run.

Sources for Further Reading

This is a rare time; people are usually not as interested as they are in 2002 in accounting, auditing, and financial statements. Accountants may be more disliked than ever, but at least they're not being ignored. Here are some sources that informed and inspired me over the years. If you were attracted to my book by its five-minute promise, perhaps you are not itching for some of the weightier volumes I am recommending. Because you can learn so much from newly discovered accounting problems—and there seem to be new ones popping up every day—you should at least be familiar with these names, because these are the best writers and commentators.

Professors Charles W. Mulford and Eugene E. Comiskey

These accounting professors have almost cornered the market on lengthy, scholarly examinations of accounting issues involving public companies over the past 20 years. Their most recent book, *The Financial Numbers Game*, came out in early 2002. I also recommend their earlier books, including *Financial Warnings* and *Guide to Financial Reporting and Analysis*.

Howard M. Schilit

Schilit is a former professor who has made a career out of evaluating the financial statements of public companies. He is

President of the Center for Financial Research and Analysis (CFRA). The CFRA has a Website, but the really good stuff is available only to the big boys, who pay $5,000 or more a year to read Schilit's findings. He is a frequent commentator on accounting issues and has written a terrific book called *Financial Shenanigans*. The second edition came out in early 2002. Not only should you get this book if you want to learn more, but you should pick up the first edition as well.

The Benjamin Graham Trail

Benjamin Graham, a Columbia Professor from 1928–1955 who counted Warren Buffett and numerous corporate chieftains as former students, revolutionized investing by focusing on fundamental financial principles revealed in corporate financial statements. Apart from the validity of many of his methods, he steered generations away from the idea that the stock market was a regulated form of gambling; he reminded that when you bought stock, you were buying a part ownership in a particular enterprise. Originally written in 1934 with Columbia colleague David Dodd, *Security Analysis* is now in its fifth edition. The periodic updates have kept the advice reasonably current. Graham also wrote *The Interpretation of Financial Statements* in 1937 and *The Intelligent Investor* in 1949 (last updated by Graham in 1973). The books show some age, especially *Financial Statements*, which has recently been reissued in its original form, but both books make excellent reading on finance.

Warren Buffett

Buffett was Graham's most famous pupil, helping popularize and advance value investing. There are numerous Buffett biographies out there, but none compare with Berkshire Hathaway's annual reports. Buffett dispenses a great deal of investment wisdom (and corny humor) in each report. Berkshire Hathaway's Website has his letters to shareholders going back to 1981.

The Dailies

The Wall Street Journal and *The New York Times*, in their extensive coverage of financial news, provide excellent commentary on current financial scandals and miscues. Also pay attention when their reporters take the trouble to pore over financial statements and remind you what's in there. That's the kind of analysis I try to do, and hope I taught you to do.

The Mags

Fortune, *Business Week*, and *Money* have a history of doing an excellent job when their reporters turn their attention to corporate financial statements, either discussing current issues or focusing on one company's financials in particular. If you aren't going to subscribe to these magazines, though I recommend you do, at least sneak a peek at the local newsstand at their tables of contents to see if they take on any accounting issues or big-company financial statements. At least have the decency (and good sense) to buy those issues.

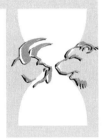

Glossary

These definitions are all accurate in an informal, I-guess-that-more-or-less-describes-the-term-as-it-applies-to-public-company-financial-statements way, but if you are studying for an accounting exam or are applying these definitions to other circumstances (for example, my definition of audit does not accurately describe what the IRS does when they want to get a closer look at you), look to more formal definitions.

The best places to find definitions of terms I haven't covered (or haven't covered in enough detail for your needs) are *www.InvestorWords.com* and any of the accounting books written by Professors Eugene Comiskey and Charles Mulford. They put glossaries at the end of each chapter of their books, but they are very thorough and pinpoint-accurate.

Accounts payable. Money a company owes for goods and services. Accounts payable appears as a current liability on the balance sheet. Increasing accounts payable improves cash flow.

Accounts receivable. Money owed to a company for goods and services. Accounts receivable appears as a current asset on the balance sheet. Increasing accounts receivables reduces cash flow.

Accrual accounting. This is the main accounting method for public companies. Under this method, a company recognizes revenue when it earns it and it recognizes expenses when it incurs them.

Accrued liabilities. Liabilities incurred by a company but not included in costs on the income statement. Under accrual accounting, liabilities would be included as costs when incurred, but if the company has not received an invoice or otherwise has an arrangement to receive goods and services but not be required to pay for them until a certain time, those amounts may be included as accrued liabilities.

American Institute of Certified Public Accountants (AICPA). Trade and professional association of the accounting profession. It issues Statement of Position (SOPs) that form a portion of GAAP. Mostly, the AICPA works to keep accounting standards and responsibilities lax.

Amortization. The periodic diminution in value of intangible assets over their useful life. The reduction in value appears as part of the costs and expenses on the income statement.

Annual report. The report disseminated to investors following a company's fiscal year. It overlaps with the version filed with the Securities & Exchange Commission, the Form 10-K. The annual report contains audited financial statements in accordance with generally accepted accounting principles.

Assets. The value of everything owned by a company. Assets appear on the balance sheet, in order of reducing liquidity.

Audit. The review of a company's financial statements, policies, and underlying support.

Audit committee. Subcommittee of a board of directors responsible for engaging and overseeing the work of the auditor. Audit committees are supposed to be composed of members independent of management.

Audit letter. The form letter provided by a company's auditor reciting that the auditor has examined the company's financial statements, policies, and underlying support, and finds that they have been prepared in conformance with generally accepted accounting principles.

Auditor. The professional hired by the audit committee of the board of directors to examine the company's financial statements and underlying data to determine if management has prepared the statements in conformance with generally accepted accounting principles.

Bad-debt reserve. Amount of receivables deducted from gross receivables on the balance sheet to represent the estimated uncollectible receivables. The bad-debt expense is the amount actually written off; the difference has to be resolved when a company abandons collection activity on particular accounts. This is another term for the **doubtful accounts reserve**.

Balance sheet. The summary of a company's assets and liabilities; what it owns and what it owes.

Basic shares outstanding. Shares of a company's stock outstanding, not counting options or other securities convertible into stock.

Big bath accounting. Pejorative term for a large one-time charge, carrying the implication that a company has timed recognition of the charge to release all the bad news at once, give the impression that it has resolved its problems, and possibly included reserves designed to artificially improve future results.

Big Five. The five accounting firms that perform 99 percent of *Fortune 500* company audits. The ranks of the Big Five have shrunk in recent years due to mergers. The five firms are Arthur Andersen, Deloitte & Touche, Ernst & Young, KPMG, and PricewaterhouseCoopers.

Black-Scholes Model. A financial model developed by Professors Black, Scholes, and Merton to determine the value of options. The formula takes into account factors such as length of the option term, exercise price, historical price, and price volatility. The model first appeared in 1973 and the professors (including Black, posthumously, who died in 1995) received the Nobel Prize for Economics in 1997.

Book value. The value of a company's tangible assets as they appear on the balance sheet (net of depreciation) minus liabilities.

Capital and surplus. A rarely used term for shareholder equity.

Capitalized. Accounting for an expenditure as an asset and depreciating or amortizing it over the life of its benefits. Expenditures are generally capitalized if they provide benefits exceeding a 12-month period.

Cash. Money in the bank plus currency. "Cash and equivalents" includes things immediately convertible into cash that might be lying around, such as cashier's checks.

Cash accounting. The alternative to accrual accounting, rarely used by public companies. Under this method, a company recognizes revenue when received and expenses when paid.

Cash flow. Cash received minus cash paid over a certain period.

Cash flow statement. Part of a company's financial statements summarizing cash received and paid over the reporting period. It is divided into activities involving operations, investments, and financing.

Cost. The amount incurred by a company in the process of producing goods and services. As an entry on the income statement, it could be separate from expenses (generally consisting of amounts incurred for things other than the production of goods and services, such as corporate overhead and marketing) or costs and expenses could be combined as one entry.

Current assets. Assets a company will turn into cash during the next 12 months. This includes cash and equivalents, marketable securities, accounts receivable, inventory, and other items.

Current liabilities. Liabilities a company must pay for during the next 12 months. This includes accounts payable, short-term debt, and other items.

Debt, short-term and long-term. Debt is money owed by a company to a financial institution or securities holders, generally distinguished from payables, which is money owed to vendors. Debt due in 12 months or less is short-term debt. All other debt is long-term debt.

Depreciation. The diminution in value of a tangible asset over its useful life. The reduction in value appears as part of the costs and expenses on the income statement.

Diluted shares outstanding. Shares of stock a company has outstanding, assuming the conversion of all securities that can be converted into common stock.

Discontinued operations. Operations within a company that it has determined to sell or close. Until the sale or closure, the financial statements will contain a separate line summarizing the results and financial condition of those operations.

Discounted cash flow. A form of valuation analysis, determining the value of certain assets or operations by estimating their future cash flows, discounted by the time-value of money. Companies are likely to use this method to support writedowns in connection with the impairment of goodwill.

Doubtful accounts reserve. Amount of receivables deducted from gross receivables on the balance sheet to represent the estimated uncollectible receivables. The doubtful accounts expense is the amount actually written off; the difference has to be resolved when a company abandons collection activity on particular accounts. This is another term for the **bad debt reserve**.

Earnings number. This is media-speak for quarterly or annual earnings per share. With the pressure to deliver news in real time, print, broadcast, and Internet reports focus on one number, which could be the GAAP earnings per share or some pro forma measure. It might also be calculated using basic or diluted shares outstanding.

Earnings per share (EPS). The product of net income divided by the number of shares outstanding.

EBITDA. An alternate measure somewhere between EPS and cash flow, it stands for Earnings Before Interest, Taxes, Depreciation, and Amortization.

Equity method. This is a method of accounting for the results of operations in which a company owns less than 50 percent. On the income statement, a company's proportionate interest is reflected as minority interest.

Expense. Expenditure by a company included all in one reporting period in the cost of revenues. If a company expects to obtain the benefit of the expenditure within 12 months, the entire amount is included. For items expected to provide benefits beyond one year, the amount is capitalized.

Expensed. This term is a verb, describing the accounting treatment of expenditures not capitalized but included all at once in the cost of revenues, (for example, "AOL finally expensed its marketing costs starting in 1997," or "I expensed that sucker with a Number Two pencil and a staple").

Financial Accounting Standards Board (FASB). Seven-person board given the responsibility by the Securities & Exchange Commission to develop Statements of Financial Accounting Standands (SFAS) and other pronouncements of generally accepted accounting principles.

Financial statement. Tables summarizing the results of operations and financial condition of a company during a particular reporting period. The financial statement generally consists of the income statement, balance sheet, and cash flow statement.

Financing cash flow. A section of the cash flow statement that describes the cash received and paid for financing activities such as the purchase and sale or stock, debt, or other securities.

Finished goods. This is the component of inventory in which all a company's work (other than selling and shipping) is complete.

FIFO. This is an acronym for "first-in, first-out," a method of inventory valuation.

Footnotes. The text following a company's financial statements that provides additional information on, among other things, significant accounting policies, the effect of accounting changes, acquisitions and divestitures, stock options, employee benefit plans, composition of debt, and any special charges taken during the reporting period.

Form 10-K. The annual report required by the Securities & Exchange Commission. It must be filed within 90 days of the end of the fiscal year. The Form 10-K overlaps substantially with the annual report, although the annual report tends to be a more polished document because it is sent to investors.

Form 10-Q. The quarterly report required by the Securities & Exchange Commission. It must be filed within 45 days of the end of the quarter. Companies also issue news releases, usually before the Form 10-Q filing deadline, announcing quarterly results. These releases are filed with the SEC, but it does not regulate their content. News releases can highlight pro forma results and omit footnote information and the cash-flow statement. Neither the Form 10-Q nor the news release requires audited quarterly results.

Generally accepted accounting principles (GAAP). The sum of all pronouncements regarding the way companies are supposed to present their financial results. GAAP can come from the SEC, the FASB, or the AICPA. In case of conflict, SEC and FASB interpretations control over AICPA interpretations.

Goodwill. Intangible asset representing the price paid for assets above their tangible asset value. In modern corporate mergers, goodwill is always a consideration because, as an asset, it has a designated useful life and has to be written down, adding to the cost of revenues and reducing net income. As of July 2001, goodwill would no longer be amortized but would be evaluated annually for impairment and written down based on the results of that evaluation by the company.

Gross margin. Revenues minus the cost of revenues.

Income statement. This portion of the financial statement describes the results of operations during the reporting period, listing the revenues earned by the company and the costs incurred. The bottom-line number is net income, which is usually expressed as earnings per share.

Initial public offering (IPO). The initial sale of shares of a company to the public. Subsequent sales of shares to the public are called secondary offerings.

Institutional investors. Professional investors responsible for managing the money of pension funds, mutual funds, and high net-worth individuals.

Intangible assets. An asset that does not have a tangible value on the balance sheet. Examples of intangible assets include goodwill, patents, and trademarks.

Inventory. Components of a company's products (consisting of raw materials, work-in-progress, and finished goods) that have not yet been sold. Inventory appears as an asset on the balance sheet.

Investing cash flow. Cash received or paid by a company in connection with investment activities, including capital spending and purchase and sales of securities and assets.

Investments. The purchase of something by a company expected to increase in value or allow it to produce goods and services. In this context, property, plant, and equipment is an investment. Alternately, investments are considered separate from operations. In that context, an investment would be the purchase of a security or some other receipt representing a company's interest in something other than its own operations.

Investor relations. This is the name of the department within a public company that issues news releases about earnings, coordinates relations between the company and the media and shareholders, and responds to shareholder requests for information. Most companies' investor-relations departments have an Internet presence, so investors can e-mail companies and obtain information online.

Liabilities. An obligation incurred by a company. This can include debts, payables, and expected future losses.

LIFO. This is an acronym for "last-in, first-out," a method of inventory valuation.

Look-through earnings. A measure of earnings developed by Warren Buffett of Berkshire Hathaway to give stockholders an idea of Berkshire's pro rata share of operating earnings of public companies in which Berkshire owned minority interests.

Management's discussion and analysis of operations (MD&A). The MD&A is the text portion of the periodic report describing a company's operations (appearing before the financial statements).

Market capitalization. The value of a company, determined by multiplying its stock price by the number of shares outstanding.

Marketable securities. Securities owned by a company that can easily be converted to cash. Usually, this means that they trade on public markets, meaning their value can fluctuate but liquidity is assured.

Net income. The product of revenues minus all costs and taxes. This is the bottom line number on the income statement, though investors recognize it more readily when it is divided by the number of shares outstanding, to create earnings per share.

Net operating loss (NOL). Prior losses that a company can recognize to offset future gains for tax purposes.

Off-balance-sheet transactions. Transactions in which a company seeks access to capital without incurring a liability to the entire company and/or having such a liability appear on the company's balance sheet. Off-balance-sheet transactions include transfers of assets to special purpose entities, synthetic and operating leases, and unused guarantees or extensions of credit.

Operating cash flow. Cash received and paid in connection with the company's operations. Net income is adjusted by changes in a company's working capital to determine operating cash flow. Increases in current assets, such as accounts receivable and inventory, reduce cash flow. Non-cash reductions in earnings, such as depreciation and amortization, increase cash flow. Increases in current liabilities, such as accounts payable, increase cash flow.

Pension income. Returns on money invested by a company's pension plan in excess of benefits paid and costs of operation. Because of smoothing of actual returns, the returns used for pension income reflect a combination of actual returns and assumed rates of return. Although a trustee controls the pension assets and companies are not allowed access to that money (not even the excess above expected benefits to be paid), the yearly excess of returns minus costs and benefits paid counts toward net income, usually as a reduction in the cost of income.

Pension plan. A retirement plan offered as an employment benefit. With the development of numerous types of tax-advantaged retirement savings, the traditional pension plan has been replaced at many companies. Because of its long use as an employment benefit, however, especially in unionized companies, the largest pension plans belong to large, mature companies such as General Motors and the successors to the old American Telephone & Telegraph. IBM and GE also have huge pension plans.

Pooling of interests. Accounting method for certain mergers eliminated in July 2001. Under a pooling merger, the parties combined assets and recorded no goodwill (and no subsequent goodwill amortization against earnings).

Prepaid expenses. This is an asset consisting of expenses paid but not yet incurred. A security deposit or retainer fee are examples of prepaid expenses.

Pro forma results. Presentation of financial results in a method other than GAAP. Companies generally issue pro forma results to show the results from operations excluding items they consider irrelevant to operations or continuing results. Companies are allowed to present such results along with GAAP results. In news releases, those companies usually emphasize the pro forma results.

Property, plant and equipment (PPE). A non-current asset on the balance sheet, consisting of the company's investment in these items. The entry usually includes the gross amount of the investment, the amount of depreciation through the reporting period, and the net remaining value.

Purchase method. Accounting method for mergers in which one company acquires another. The acquirer adds the target's assets and liabilities to its balance sheet. The purchase price in excess of the net tangible asset value is listed as goodwill, an intangible asset on the balance sheet. As of July 2001, all mergers must be accounted for as purchase-method mergers, the pooling-of-interest method having been eliminated.

Quarterly report. Publicly available version of a company's financial results, usually issued in the form of a news release about three weeks after the end of a quarter. It includes the same results as the Form 10-Q, but the quarterly report is usually presented first, and the quarterly report differs in presentation.

Raw materials. Component of inventory consisting of purchases of materials by a company that have not been converted into goods.

Regulation S-X. Securities & Exchange Commission regulation describing the format for quarterly (Form 10-Q) and annual (Form 10-K) reports.

Reserve. A separate account—generally a bookkeeping entry rather than segregating cash—maintained for the purpose of estimating, then comparing actual results against the estimate, an anticipated liability. Companies issuing credit typically maintain a reserve for doubtful accounts. Companies restructuring operations announce up front the amount the restructuring will cost, establish a reserve account in that amount, then charge restructuring expenses against that reserve.

Restructuring charge. General name for several kinds of one-time charges taken in anticipation of expenses to restructure operations. These charges can include spending money in the near future for things such as severance and the costs of closing down certain operations. They can also include recognition that prior money spent will not result in a return to the company, writing off the value of assets such as inventory and goodwill.

Retained earnings. The total amount of a company's earnings minus dividends.

Retirement plan. General name for company obligations to workers for retirement and post-retirement benefits. That can include pension plans, health insurance, and anything else a company has agreed to provide former workers as an employment benefit.

Revenue. The total amount of goods and services provided by a company during a reporting period. Revenue appears as the first line of the income statement.

Revenue recognition. Accounting decisions made by a company, conforming to GAAP, about when it can count goods and services as revenue. Under accrual accounting, a company can recognize revenue before it receives payment.

Securities Act of 1933. Early law federalizing securities regulation. The 1933 Act focused on securities offerings by companies.

Securities and Exchange Act of 1934. The main source of federal regulation of securities markets. The 1934 Act focused on behavior by market participants and disclosure obligations of public companies after completion of securities offerings, for as long as a company's stock trades publicly. The 1934 Act also established the SEC to develop regulations pursuant to the principles announced in the Act and enforce them.

Securities and Exchange Commission (SEC). Federal agency created in 1934 to regulate the securities markets, establishing and enforcing regulations consistent with Congress's laws on the subject.

Selling, general and administrative expense (SG&A). Expenses not involved in the physical production of goods and services. These expenses include corporate overhead and marketing expenses.

Shareholder equity. An entry as a liability on the balance sheet, this represents the difference between the value of all assets minus all liabilities.

Spin off. Transaction in which a company registers shares in one or more of its subsidiaries, and issues a stock dividend to shareholders, representing their pro rata share of the subsidiary. Following the spin off, the subsidiary's stock trades publicly and it operates as an independent company.

Staff Accounting Bulletin (SAB). Accounting pronouncement by the Securities & Exchange Commission, it forms part of GAAP.

Standard & Poors 500 Index (S&P 500). Index based on the stock prices of 500 large companies. The investment community generally views the S&P 500 as a proxy for how the stock market as a whole is performing.

Statement of Financial Accounting Standards (SFAS). Accounting pronouncement by the Financial Accounting Standards Board, it forms part of GAAP.

Statement of Position (SOP). Accounting pronouncement by the American Institute of Certified Public Accountants, it forms part of GAAP.

Stock options. Securities giving the holder the right (but not the obligation) to purchase a company's stock at a certain price, exercisable over a certain time. Companies have increasingly made stock options available to employees as a form of compensation. Typically, the options will give the employee the right to purchase a company's stock at its price on the issuing date or at a price based on some formula taking its past and current price into account. The option is then exercisable over several years, giving the employee an opportunity to profit from increases in the price of a company's stock.

Stock split. Declaration by a company that it will increase its outstanding shares, issuing new shares on a pro rata basis to its shareholders. Typically the sign of a company with a rising stock price, the split has no effect on operations or ownership.

Tangible asset value. This is another term for book value, the value of a company's hard assets (excluding intangibles such as trade names and goodwill, if they appear on the balance sheet).

Tracking stock. Issuance of a security that does not represent an ownership interest in certain company assets or operations, but pays a dividend or gives the owner a segregated ownership in a company's assets (though not necessarily the ones the subject of the tracking stock) based on the results of certain operations. The operations remain wholly-owned by the company, but the stock reflects the value of those operations, because the shareholders receive a dividend based on the operations' results or have some right to an equivalent amount of corporate assets.

Unamortized. The portion of intangible assets not yet deducted from the balance sheet based on amortization schedules.

Weighted average price inventory. This is a method of valuing inventory, combining components obtained at different times for different prices to determine an average price.

Work-in-progress. A component of inventory, between raw materials and finished goods.

Working capital. This is the total of current assets (cash, marketable securities, accounts receivable, inventory, etc.) minus current liabilities (accounts payable, short-term debt, etc.).

Index

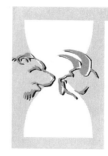

About the Author

Michael Craig is a retired lawyer who now writes about business, finance, investing, law, and politics from Scottsdale, Arizona. He is the author of *The 50 Best (and Worst) Business Deals of All Time*.